Explore the birth of freestyle through the life of Eric Hymans, Australian skiing's original wild man, from skibum to number one to recluse. Son of a legendary ski pioneer, Eric won two Australian mogul championships after starting Falls Creek's iconic *Team Red* with a bunch of talented athletes. This gang was instrumental to the explosion of freestyle skiing in the 80s. Establishing the *Summit Masters* they planted seeds for freedom.

Born to fly uncovers the circumstances that made game-changing performers. Plus the relationships that saw an enigmatic character refine his art and ultimately fall from grace. Epic times at the forefront of extreme, along with the perils that exist. Laced with historical significance and a refreshing candour, this story delivers lessons and wisdom from a classic freeride elder.

Eric Hymans from grommet to elder.

'From my generation, Eric Hymans was one of the real characters of the Falls Creek community.'

Steven Lee – Champion skier / Olympian

'Some very good writing and sensational memories... Nice work, you've captured an era.'

Jim Darby – Editor of The Ski Mag

'A truly great presentation of a deeply passionate and complex friend. You have done him proud with your words... and have managed in the same breath, to give some honour to many people who shared his journey... not an easy feat.'

Katie Steven - Champion Team Red Skier

'Born to Fly is a beautifully crafted portrait of Eric Hymans. It shows the sheer gravity of success Hymans' achieved and the difficulty of maintaining such success. Raw, honest, and emotional. 'Born to Fly' highlights not only the rise of freestyle skiing, but the journey of its foremost athlete. Readers will be captivated and inspired.'

Ashley Pascual - Senior Editor at Austin Macauley

for Kyle

Born to fly

Copyright © Peter Corney 2018

Biographical

Although based on a real skier, the author makes no reference to other worlds, times or realities. While familiar people, places and historic events assist a sense of realism - this story is considered imaginary. The language used is from a singular viewpoint, sensationalised for reader enjoyment, education and spiritual inspiration.

Other than standard media review, reproduction, distribution or referencing in any way, shape or form, or by any means, requires explicit approval from the author. Proudly an epic profit-share production.

Internationally eco-friendly.

Independently produced by

Epicscope
PO Box 48
Falls Creek
Vic. 3699
Australia

www.epicscope.com.au

ISBN: 978-0-9581930-4-7

FRONT COVER - Eric daffy above the Frying Pan Inn.
BACK COVER - Team Red ruling the Summit of Falls Creek 1986.
The stylish leader (holding perfect form) is captain / coach Eric Hymans, followed by Mark Steven, Kent Dowding and Marcus Lovett - Bill Bachman photo

PHOTOS - Hymans family, Robin Bayly-Jones, Jeep Novak, Mike Haid, Katie Steven, Bill Bachman, Damien Pierce, Kerri Darby, Tim Patrick, Tony McLaughlin, Justin Field, Graeme Cox, Charlie Brown, Trevor Avedissian.

Born to fly

FREESTYLE
ski roots

peter corney

ERIC 10

LE SKI BUM 17

TEAM RED 39

FALLS CREEK 55

GROWING UP 71

BIRTH OF FREESTYLE 85

LOCAL KNOWLEDGE 101

RESORT POLITICS 117

SKI BROTHERHOOD 135

VERBIER CONNECTION 157

SUMMIT MASTERS 179

APRES SKI 209

SUNSET 223

Too fast to live
Too young to die!

ERIC

I bumped into Eric Hymans in the Mount Beauty supermarket a while back. He wasn't looking so well. Approaching sixty he appeared older and I wondered what part drugs, booze and thoughts of injustice were having on his condition - things that often haunt men with colourful pasts slowly disappearing. As per standard practice I greeted Eric with a warm handshake and gentle bow of my head, acknowledging him as a 'Grand Master'. Showing genuine respect to an elder of the free-ski tribe. A fresh sparkle in his eyes put a warm glow between us as he struggled to recognise me. I got the feeling my show of respect was a rare occurrence in his latter life.

Eric was wearing an original Heartcore beanie and I motion this was our connection. 'Pea Ce,' he remembered, 'Epic Freeride, I have one of your books.' The tone in his voice shifted from struggle to something reminiscent of youth, 'Poetry for the People!' He leaned in closer and almost whispered, 'Hey, you know we are from the same spirit... I'm an original freerider.'

'Yes indeed,' I agreed, but in truth I didn't yet know the depths, complexities or achievements of Eric Hymans. I felt like a young Jedi meeting Yoda for the first time. During my thirty years visiting Falls Creek his name was always surrounded by mountain myth, rumour and innuendo. I'd heard he was a great skier, an innovative freestyler, a big party guy, and his father Bob Hymans was a pioneer of Australian skiing. Other than that, he may as well have lived in a completely different world. Except for Team Red.

When I arrived at Falls, as a budding snowboarder in the late eighties, there were no kids who had grown up snowboarding so I found inspiration in the grace and spirit of Team Red skiers. The way they dominated the hill with fluid form, their charisma and style. Summit masters. Freestyle revolution. *The Verbier Connection* ski movie was a big hit during those times and the whole scene was electric. For me there is no separation between freestylers: planks or boards or bikes, whatever - when one finds the buzz it's a beautiful thing. There is nothing better than chasing balance and then achieving it, challenging the status quo, busting down the doors to freedom, and it is in this realm that Eric and I are on common ground.

Online, Team Red photos from the eighties caught my attention. Lynne Grosse, Mark Steven, Steve Lee, Marcus Lovett, Kent Dowding and Flash are recognisable as movers and shakers in the Australian ski industry. Legendary skiers. Eric Hymans stood among them.

So what is Eric's part in all this history? I'm fascinated and post a suggestion he 'write a book', certain I'm not the only one interested in the Eric Hymans story and history of Team Red. Through the power of technology, Eric sees I'm in Beauty and invites me to visit him with a bottle of wine. 'Honour thy elders' they say, so I picked up a nice local Benjella Shiraz on the way to Eric's Lakeside Drive house. My heart was open. Eyes sparkled with anticipation.

Eric looked noticeably better than he had in the supermarket, younger even. He wanted to show me some things and the first were his tattoos. Eric peeled off his t-shirt, exposing a weathered warrior-like physique, and across his back in Thai writing are two words that mean 'balance' and 'harmony'. 'These are the foundations on which we live our lives as freeriders,' Eric explained. He then showed me his arms - on one is a Mogul Mania tattoo from freestyle skiing, that gives him a sense of commitment to that life, and on the other a Rolling Stones tongue, equally a part of who he is. These represent where Eric found his freedom. I loved the Rolling Stones and once painted a big Stones emblem on an old EH Holden back in the day, which Eric took as evidence of our shared interests.

His lounge room was unkempt in true bachelor style and the decor looked very shitty eighties. The coffee table was crowded with photo albums and scrapbooks, with a note pad on top covered in scribbled writing. Empty beer cans complemented a loaded ashtray. Above his lounge chair *The Verbier Connection* movie poster hung proudly.

I remarked that it was one of my favourite ski movies of all time, noticing Eric's name among the credits.

Eric revealed the reason for my invitation was to help him put his story together. Trevor Avedissian, the producer of *The Verbier Connection*, was working on a retrospective about the pioneers of La Glisse (extreme sports) and Eric felt inclined to share his part in that history. Eric has done just about everything except write and didn't know where to start. English is not his mother tongue as he did all of his schooling in French and picked up Australian organically from living up at Falls Creek. He can ski, ride bikes, fix cars, build stuff, and cook like a master chef, but writing - forget about it. He was too impatient at school.

I was at once both humbled and excited at the prospect of hearing Eric's life story. A little apprehensive about the work and responsibility involved to share it with the world. More than grateful to be on the radar of a Falls Creek legend, who was one of the main players during the birth of Freestyle as we know it today.

Eric's quirky resonance took me in, so I pulled out my smart phone and pressed record on the voice memo app. What transpired over a number of late nights with a few drinks, the odd smoke and some mouth watering food, is a story equally shocking as it is revealing about a life lived to the extreme. Throw in an array of tales from old friends and young onlookers of his day, and we have a fascinating read worth sharing.

Eric's journey isn't all glory. A sadness beneath the surface longs to resolve the puzzling reality of great freeriders falling through the cracks of time and space. Inherent in this tale are lessons, wisdom, and humour, from a freeride elder, about living life on your own terms, with as few regrets as possible.

This is his story as only he can see it. To give the reader a feeling for Eric's unique character, I have retained his language where possible and included certain mannerisms that made this man, and his myth, so intriguing.

Although I have reached out to as many people as possible who spent time with Eric, to gain further reflection, a lot have either fallen silent or remarked that most of Eric's life is unpublishable. He lived some pretty wild and crazy times, often controversial, and inarguably depressing on many levels. I know I must tread lightly, but as we discover the real Eric Hymans, we uncover a journey that was meant to be. This is a man with a big heart, who became a style of skier who contributed heavily to mountain culture and folklore. He is an elder who might appear to have struggled reinventing himself after skiing, but who has something profound to share.

Hearing this peculiar tale from the horse's mouth after said horse has bolted, leaves me wondering how accurate the recollections of an old freeride warrior can be? Myth is often embellishment, legend maybe also. Eric's story is about wildness of spirit rebellion, an incited revolution to live without rules or dominion.

His path laid down in a childhood many weren't there to witness, with a soundtrack that only punk could adequately grace.

While living his fair share of sunny days, there have been increasing numbers of dark days. Inherent in Eric's sharing of his life, is a refreshing candour in the open hearted passing of knowledge. Embellished or stranger than fiction no matter, we aren't about to let the truth get in the way of a damn good yarn. With any luck more of Eric's friends, family and skiing fraternity will come forward after reading this version of events to contribute further insight. Then we might fill any gaps, answer unanswered questions, and expand the legend of freestyle skiing's pioneering days for the benefit of future generations.

Hang onto your heartstrings ladies and gentlemen, this is the Eric Hymans story - *Born to Fly*.

Eric and Brigitte Hymans, on the road to La Plagne France 1979 - BJ photo

LE SKI BUM

In 1975 Eric Hymans arrived at Falls Creek to work like a slave in his father's Four Seasons chalet. Bob Hymans was an Australian skiing pioneer who had been doing back-to-back winters in Europe and Australia for many years, mainly as a ski instructor but also in hospitality, ski patrol and resort development. Although Eric had skied from a young age, it was the first time he would get to ski every day for a whole snow season. There was great change under foot and a new style of skiing had just been born. They called it hot-dogging, where skiers attacked mogul runs to catch air off the bumps. Traditionally the popular forms of skiing were racing around gates or cross-country touring. Eric was into this new wave and so began a love affair that would influence the course of skiing history.

As per the times, there wasn't much work at Falls Creek during the summer. Most of the residents would relocate at a beach or travel to Northern Hemisphere destinations for more snow. There was something very special about skiing for Eric so he joined the migration north. Bob was now in his fifties and had lived a hard life, naturally his skiing was slowing down. While Eric was seventeen and of course his skiing was speeding up, he had also been exposed to hardship from his parents' separation.

In their hearts they both felt they had to care for each other. Things were difficult for the Hymans in many respects, but they counted their lucky stars every time they found themselves standing on top of a mountain. When the winter snow melted in Australia they made the annual pilgrimage to Europe.

Eric's first solo season was in a French ski town called La Plagne, where Bob had taken him before. Travelling with Robin 'BJ' Bayly-Jones they flew into Amsterdam on one-way tickets. While checking out all the sights, the boys were chased out of the red light district for window-shopping hookers without wanting to pay for them.

Eric had friends everywhere and they made their way to his mum's place near Brussels. BJ loved meeting Eric's European family, really beautiful people who were warm, friendly and very accommodating.

From there they caught a train to Geneva and went shopping for the latest ski gear. Both scored a pair of new technology Hanson Hummer moulded plastic ski boots. That became famous as the style storm troopers wore in the original Star Wars movie, released in cinemas that year to rave reviews. The boys felt high-tech like they were from outer space. To stretch their money they slept in train stations, using their ski bags as pillows.

When finally arriving at their destination in France, they managed to stash their gear in a construction site that was closed for the winter. For warmth they slept in a hotel fire escape basement for a few weeks while trying to find work.

Keen to explore, they emptied their pockets on tram tickets to ski the mountains. After money ran out things got desperate and they begrudgingly decided to leave.

A local lady, who picked them up hitch hiking out of town, took a liking to these handsome lads. After dropping them off at the nearest train station, she called her parents and organised two ski-bum jobs in her family's hotel. When she went to find them again they were nowhere to be found, but their ski gear was outside the station. She left a note on their bags with the good news and directions, signed with a love heart.

The boys had ducked into a nearby pub to drown their sorrows. When they eventually found her note they couldn't believe their luck, skipping with joy as they found their way. Eric was given a bar job speaking French while BJ did cleaning. The restaurant management worked them to the bone with no time off. Once it became clear that their pay was next to nothing they got outta there. The whole point was to go skiing as much as possible.

Like a lot of classic skibum journeys, they eventually hit the real jackpot and scored work for an on-mountain restaurant, with accommodation and lift tickets provided. This enabled them to ski everyday. Like Sherpas, they carried all the supplies in and rubbish out on their skis. With big L-shaped aluminium frame backpacks they lugged water containers, gas canisters and everything the restaurant used. Often carrying forty kilograms on their backs while skiing.

To ease their workload, Eric had the bright idea to drop the water containers off a chairlift that went near their restaurant. Then they would get to free-ski down. When he tried it for the first time, his backpack got caught on the hinged seat and the weight of the water flipped him off the chair. Luckily knee-deep powder snow softened his six-metre fall. Then the water container took off down the slope and nearly killed some people, who were skiing on the piste below. Eric was always looking for the most efficient way to do things and often made everyone laugh (or cringe) in the process.

Being a Sherpa was Eric's job for a couple of seasons during Euro winters and one can imagine it helped refine his skiing dramatically. Deep in the Alps the mountains of this area stand like giants, demanding both respect and skill from its inhabitants. The boys naturally became better skiers and Eric especially wanted to impress his father.

Returning to Falls Creek through the change of seasons, they repeated the process of skiing everyday when snow was on the ground. Eric had become a ski bum. He joined an openhearted lifestyle that was imperative to a new breed of youth who did things differently. The offspring of war-torn generations were becoming liberated. Everything revolved around freedom and exploring what was possible.

Goofing around with BJ and John Falkiner during the winter of '77, Eric was the first to throw a front flip on skis and landed it first go. Nobody was doing those moves and he decided to try it for something different, a new idea.

Eric Hymans front flipping with John Falkiner. Falls Creek 1977

Not knowing he was becoming one of the hot dogs, Eric had started to turn heads. Many regarded him as the most charismatic and flamboyant character during those times.

Eric was an amusing personality, especially when he learnt English. He used to say, 'My feet fingers are frozen!' when his toes were cold, because that was the direct translation from French. There were also some funny tales of crew teaching Eric the local lingo through pick up lines. All the boys laughed their heads off as Eric approached women with stupid phrases they set him up with, then Eric would pull it off and invariably take a lady home.

The following year, using one of these hilarious pick up lines, he hooked up with a remarkable surfer girl by the name of Lynne Grosse. They began a romantic entanglement that, before the end, would take skiing to another level and help produce champions.

By 1979 Eric's skiing had improved immensely and a twist of fate would push him further. Gebi Auderer, who managed the original Molony's ski hire at Falls Creek, decided to rally support for Eric to compete on the Peter Stuyvesant (cigarette company) Freestyle Tour. Gebi knew great skiing when he saw it and helping Eric was a way to promote their resort. Eric's skiing might never have been recognised without this good fortune. There was Olympian Malcolm Milne, the first Australian skier to win a World Cup downhill event in 1969, a big name. Steven Lee was making his mark in ski racing. Then along came Eric Hymans flying the flag for Falls Creek freestyle.

Gary Braid, a full-on ocker abalone diver staying at Four Seasons, volunteered to drive Eric to New South Wales for his first comp. They had skied together and Gary loved Eric's style. The whole way he raved Eric up, 'Nobody got a hope against you mate, ya gotta believe that - you are the best skier out there!' Eric fought off his insecurities and allowed himself to be convinced. After they arrived to where the competitors were staying in Thredbo, Gary kept preaching about Eric's prowess on skis and wigged everyone out with his Aussie righteousness. The American pro skiers especially figured Eric was indeed someone to be feared on a mogul course.

By the end of the competition, Eric had scored first Australian and fourth International. Behind Canadians Greg Athans (2 x Mogul World Champ '76, '78), John Eaves (6 x World Championships '77-'80, Aerials and Combined) and Murray Cluff (Canadian Champion and World Cup performer). Joe Kellie, who later took the tour title for locals, was second Australian and eleventh International. Eric was up there with the best in the world, clearly one of the greatest freestyle skiers in Australia at the time. Who would have thought a decade later his life would spiral out of control.

Protests began about Eric's origin, with his French accent, so he had to prove his citizenship to be considered Australia's best. The bickering was disconcerting since Eric had held an Australian passport since June 1958. He didn't get a trophy but he got a four hundred and thirty five dollar cheque for his twenty-five second performance.

Which in those days was a 'fuck load' of money due to the average wage being around three dollars an hour. Eric was suddenly a professional athlete and figured he might as well keep doing these events to make dollars from what he loved.

For a period of time Eric Hymans would make a big impression in Australian skiing. Looking back he reckoned believing in your abilities is a sure way to go to the next level. One of his more profound beliefs would lie dormant until later in this story.

He continued to give stand out performances and placed second to Joe Kellie in Mount Buller. His home event at Falls Creek was cancelled due to bad weather, after organisers were declined the use of a machine to clean up heavy snow and push the jumps. Eric was a little embarrassed about the lack of support. To make amends he went out of his way to make sure the visiting freestylers had the time of their lives. Leading competitors into his favourite skiing on the Summit and Eagle Ridge. Arcing into the Slot cornice for his signature re-entry, boosting Rocket Launcher over Cabbage Patch and dropping his favourite rock lines under Eagle chair. The storm riding was fun and there was a lot of aspects around the village bowl that people hadn't considered until they skied with Eric.

Peter Stuyvesant personally came to the event and the tour party at the Frying Pan was voted the best of that entire season. A token wet t-shirt competition broadcast live on closed circuit televisions around the venue, for everyone to view the 'nippley titties' in a packed house.

Chantal and Eric Hymans, Frying Pan pirate party, Falls Creek 1978

These times were wild. The pinnacle of that evening was the then current tour leader getting naked on stage with the girls. After stuffing his genitals into a schooner glass he proceeded to launch a near perfect heli off the stage and into the crowd. Everyone erupted. 'At least Falls Creek knew how to party!'

Eric looked into joining the Freestyle World Tour fulltime, but a previous customs indiscretion would prevent his access to North America, where the bulk of the events operated. His admirers expressed disappointment. As a consolation, Eric was invited to model in a film shoot for Victorian Ski Association promotions. The doors of World Tour opportunity might have slammed shut but there were other options.

Eric returned to work in the kitchen at night and hid his disappointment about missing a spot on the World Tour. In between seasons he 'busted a gut' on various construction jobs to fund ski travel. The year he became recognised as a gun in Australian Freestyle, he headed back to Europe with his girlfriend for more on-mountain experience.

Lynne Grosse remembered starting out skiing with Eric in jeans and leather jackets and having to save every penny to travel. Eric liked to live in the now and share everything with everyone. He had a short attention span and was definitely a loose cannon, but the ski bum life was simple: save for an airfare; stop over in Asia on the way; find a chalet to sleep in for winter; score lift tickets and lock into survival mode to eat and enjoy. No bills or debts.

Being classic ski bums they slept in airports, train stations and bus depots, and were willing to crash in any nook or cranny if need be, with the hope of one day competing on the Europa Cup ski circuit. There were no coaches, money, or team sponsorships (let alone sports psychology). What was cool though, about all the hard work and leaps of faith, was that there was always something fun going on to keep their spirits up.

When Lynne and Eric arrived at La Plagne in France, they went to a resort Eric knew about where everything is connected through corridors. Big tunnels from underground car parking to everything imaginable, so guests didn't have to walk through the snow. That place had an indoor swimming pool with gaps in the wall so you could swim to an outside pool situated right next to a ski run. Eric and Lynne would jump out of the pool to roll around in the snow then get back in. They were free and figuring it all out moment to moment. Simply going with the flow.

Through epic times meeting new people, they ended up in a *maison partagée* (share house) high on a mountainside above the snow line. It was a cold and humble existence. Whatever people in the house earned all went straight into a communal jar, with any expenses coming out of that jar. They met locals and received gifts of cured meat and cheese from farmers down the valley. Some of the crew would road trip to Amsterdam every month to score other supplies. They ran a roster to collect wood, or ski to the *boulangerie* (bakery) for bread each day.

Eric Hymans, La Plagne France 1980

Taking it in turns to cook warm oatmeal porridge for breakfast and serve up chickpea and vegetable soups for dinner. Lunch was often simply a *baguette* (long bread roll) and a block of cheese shared among them.

Every day they trekked out into the high alpine areas, above the tree line, to ski epic mountains and jump off wind-lips or cliffs for airtime. They were always pushing each other's form to constantly refine and redefine their skiing abilities. Looking back at their tracks to see who left the cleanest lines. Style was everything.

Eric often thinks about the uniqueness of Lynne Grosse. She came to Falls Creek from South Australia in the winter of 1978, having never seen snow before, and they skied together. She had surfed and done gymnastics and was a natural, so by '79 they travelled to Europe for more experience. The year they came back, Lynne became the Australian women's ski champion. In two years or a year and a half that was amazing. For Eric it wasn't amazing to be the champion because his mum put him on skis when he was young. To Eric skiing is like walking, he has always known how to do it. Eric was maybe the first person Lynne skied with and they skied together all the time.

Ralph Storey, who was a ski patroller in the seventies, remembered seeing Lynne follow Eric around and commented on how good she was skiing. Eric told him she had only been skiing for a week. Ralph was dumbfounded. People skied with Eric and the improvement through being around his energy allowed them to reach new levels.

In La Plagne, Eric returned to his job as a Sherpa, carrying supplies on his skis. His trusty L-shaped aluminium frame backpack secured heavy loads again. He was often paid in food and drinks. Lynne meanwhile scored a job cleaning chalets a day or two each week. Their whole life together was living in ski boots.

Taking the garbage to the village *poubelle* (rubbish collection) was always done below a chair lift, down a bump run the resort used when they held competitions. Sometimes bags would come loose and there'd be a garage sale (as we say in Australia) or a trail of destruction that they'd struggle to clean up. People would watch them and laugh uncontrollably.

An American guy had an apartment overlooking that run and saw Eric and Lynne ski past every day. Eventually he found them in a cafe and immediately invited them both to be in a ski movie with Jean-Claude Killy, who was considered the best skier on Earth at the time. Eric was blown away. These little kids from a hill in Australia, invited to ski with the best in the world. That first movie they took part in was aptly named *Le ski bum*.

Jean-Claude Killy was an orthodox skier with a lifetime of experience, who skied for the K2 factory team. He had travelled to Falls Creek before and actually met Eric's father Bob. Jean-Claude had a traditional style but when he saw Eric ski he was impressed. He and Eric talked about techniques and both agreed Eric's style encapsulated a different way to ski.

Eric Hymans, Jean-Claude Killy, Henri Duvillard, Lynne Grosse
La Plagne France 1980

Through Jean-Claude, Eric and Lynne got insight into the marketing strategies driving ski business. Progressively, the flow of free ski gear through casual hook ups increased. Now recognised as some of Australia's best skiers, their lives evolved fast to become all about skiing.

Eric dreamt of being given prototype skis direct from the factory, to test and evaluate. Visiting his sponsor's production plant every year to pick out what he wanted, whatever style he liked, but with a stealth white top sheet and black base marked only by custom specifications hand engraved underfoot. Eric's responsibility would be in giving feedback on how new models performed during various carving techniques and different ways of jumping, bumps, whatever. Ski companies are constantly changing things and looking for new technology, so Eric fantasised about becoming part of that process.

Bob Hymans had been heading back to Europe for over two decades. When he retired from skiing he preferred time alone at their family cottage in the South of France or renting a chalet near Eric. All along their journey together they were constantly clashing through a love / hate relationship between old school and new, father and son, master and apprentice.

Bob spent time as a prisoner of war and an undiagnosed neurosis, or post-traumatic stress syndrome, was at odds with Eric's unconventional free spirit. Still, in many ways it might have been viewed that Bob facilitated his son to live how he himself couldn't during that age.

Few people would know that Eric and his father had even an inkling of respect for each other. Behind closed doors Eric would care for Bob in times of need and in a weird or old-fashioned way Bob did the same for Eric. It felt to Eric that he was always overshadowed by Bob, so he didn't like living or travelling with his father unless he had to. Back at Falls Creek it was inevitable when Bob kicked Eric out of the nest. Barry Lawther, who built The Hub and later Snowdrift Lodge, knew how harsh Bob was and helped Eric get a cooking job at the Man Restaurant. It was time to spread his wings and focus on himself.

People were constantly telling Eric how good he was skiing, but he didn't feel like a great skier, he wanted to get better. He craved perfection, trained frenetically and worked hard to try and prove himself to his father. His time on skis was completely self-absorbed in the moment, and he searched deep inside his soul to power the spark of creativity that made him stand out.

He continued performing on the Peter Stuyvesant Freestyle Tour in Australia and earned another top spot in the developing Australian Freestyle Championships of '81. A newspaper clipping in one of Eric's scrapbooks reported:

> Probably the most exciting run of the day was by Australian Eric Hymans who beat all other Aussies to place 5th overall. But the World Cup boys showed their expertise by placing one, two and three in both runs. Frank Beddor (2nd in World Cup moguls) was overall winner with Murray Cluff 2nd and Rick Bowie 3rd.

Eric's surviving badges

Eric knew if he had more experience he could beat these guys and even become a world champion. Competitions aren't for everyone but Eric was good at them. Frustrations cut deep. The reality of being an outsider in the full professional realm helped him become the life of the party. The Hymans are a big-hearted bunch and showing everyone a good time was part of Eric's DNA. Returning to Europe, where his command of the language and culture complemented his growing experience in the Alps, was a no brainer. He still kicked arse in a few places.

Jarrah Kurth recalled a fireside tale about Eric ski racing against Swiss and German pros. All these lycra clad racers were stretching and sharpening their edges at the top of the course. When Eric Hymans rocked up to the gate smoking a joint. He took a long hit and blew it toward the stiffs to suggest something like, 'Give it a rest fellas - none of you have a hope!' then proceeded to win the event.

These stories paint a fascinating personality. For a time Eric did anything he put his mind to. Which influenced a number of skiers who ended up dominating freestyle.

Brigitte reminisced about watching her brother ski. Their family nicknamed him rubber legs because his legs were so flexible, moving like elastic bands when he was going down the moguls. He was jumping, flying, dancing, enjoying it in such a fluid way it was so beautifully effortless, magical, it was grace... that's when you're doing it to perfection, and that's the key and the beauty in any sport, in art, in everyday life for anyone. That's when you've really got it!

In 1982, his father told Eric to NOT even think about going to the Australian Skiing Championships because Steve Lee was going and he didn't drink, didn't smoke and trained all the time. Steve had become a real athlete so Eric had no hope. Eric told Bob that he was going no matter what! As things turned out, Eric won and Steve Lee came second (in freestyle not racing). Another newspaper clipping stated:

> In what was a very close competition, spectators saw Eric Hymans, 1981 Australian mogul champion, wrestle victory from Australian Alpine team member, Steven Lee. Finishing a close third was long time racer and freestyler Gary Holt.

That year Eric also won a slalom event as well. Steve usually dominated the racecourses and went on to be one of Australia's greatest international exports. Eric won his second national mogul championship as the free bird, cut-loose, go for it, in the zone. He had developed a raw natural style with unique flare that allowed him to flow like water down the fall line of a mogul run.

When Eric got home, Bob had left a case of champagne on Eric's bed, as a way to say congratulations. Bob would never praise his son verbally, so Eric got drunk after enjoying good success in competitions up to that point. While things would begin to take a sideways spiral, his influence among the skiing fraternity became legendary. Something had started that would change the face of the Australian ski industry forever.

Eric holding his skis highest, Guthega 1982

Lynne Grosse, Eric Hymans, Steven Lee, Peter Williams, Andy Thomas and Flash in front. 1982 - Mike Haid photo

TEAM RED

In Australia at Falls Creek, Eric dreamt of inspiring young ones to ski and even coach them, so he did a ski instructors clinic. In the early eighties he was regarded as one of Australia's best freestyle skiers. Astonishingly, at the end of the clinic, the head instructor wanted to fail him.

All the trainee instructors were sitting in a classroom after their course. With the big Austrian kahuna reading grades, saying such and such passed, such and such passed, 'Eric Hymans, oh, just passed, you've got a problem with your hip angulation,' totally dissing Eric's skiing style. A long time friend, who had actually taken up skiing because of how Eric skied, put his hand on Eric's shoulder and said, 'Don't worry about it mate!' Eric felt like challenging them all to a slalom race to see who really knew how to ski, but bit his tongue instead, thinking, 'Austrians are such arrogant skiers.'

When he went home he relayed the outcome to Bob, who picked up the phone to the ski school director to complain. The poor grade was because Eric was an unorthodox skier who didn't follow the rulebook, breaking tradition when nobody else was skiing that way. Freestyle skiing was not yet fully accepted in the early eighties and Eric didn't fit into the ski school mould.

While cooking at the Man Restaurant, Eric started promoting his food out on the hill to bring people in for dinner. It worked so well it became a sponsorship of sorts and badges were put on jackets, vouches printed for free beer. Lynne earned similar support from the Sundance Inn, another great social establishment of the day. Bringing everyone together at the best after-ski bars was a natural part of sharing the magic. Meeting people in lift lines was perfect to spread the word. Then the idea came to start a Falls Creek Freestyle Team, with Eric and Lynne joining sponsors for the benefit of the whole community, but they needed more than two skiers to make a team.

Peter Williams had returned from a back-to-back winter in the States, skiing with World Cup freestylers, and was performing in the bumps alongside Eric. Pete was in. The word went out and it also excited Steve Lee and Andy Thomas. (A bit of trivia is how Andy went on with partner Janet to create Jandys Innovative Sports in 1986, which pushed the forefront of ski clothing for over 30 years. Their Pure Mountain range fitted out crew for the PyeongChang Winter Olympics in 2018.) Andy was an exceptional ballet skier back in the day, who had connections with Richard Braithwaite, a ski gear distributer in Sydney. They managed to negotiate a bunch of red one-piece suits along with Volkl skis, Lange boots and Uvex goggles, which remained unsold from the previous season. This got the crew looking and feeling like a real professional team. It was the very first sponsorship of its type to occur on Australian snow.

Steve was already on the national race team, so never actually donned a red suit for freestyle. The others skied bumps together, earning hoots and hollers. Without any formality they went to competitions in the early eighties and kicked arse. Steve's mum Noelene was integral to getting things moving. With a genuine camaraderie and community spirit growing stronger around Falls, as people who remember those days always comment with fond recollection.

Randy Wieman, a former champion freestyle pioneer, nicknamed them Team Red during a competition practice because they were all hot skiers in red suits. Team Red certainly had a better ring to it than Team Falls Creek so the endearment stuck.

Katie and Mark Steven grew up skiing at Falls Creek and Katie especially skied a lot with Steve, Eric and Lynne. When they got out of school and wanted to do freestyle they joined Team Red. Kent Dowding, Tracy Lee, Andy Kelly, and Marcus Lovett also joined the mix at various stages, as word spread about who were the greatest skiers on the hill each season. It was all pretty loose and these friends came and went from Team Red, but for the duration of the eighties and into the nineties, three generations of this gang would become synonymous with Falls Creek.

There's a jump under Eagle Chair called Red Rock because only Team Red skiers would launch off it and soar over the Summit home trail. If you were lucky enough to be on one of those chairs, when Team Red came flying underneath, it was a very special sight to behold.

BORN TO FLY

Lynne Grosse. Bill Bachman photo

TEAM RED

Mark Steven flying fresh Team Red colours - magazine advertisement 1986

The talk around the village, and back in the cities when holidaymakers returned home, was the stuff that made legends. Road trips to competitions were organised to represent Falls Creek and photo opportunities taken to promote the exciting lifestyle of skiing.

Lynne would go on to be the first woman to do a double backflip in ski aerials competition, becoming a multiple champion. Mark, Katie, Pete and Marcus also won freestyle championships in their own right. All of Team Red would stand on a podium a number of times. The notion that these personalities busted down the doors for Freestyle makes absolute sense. They were all pushing each other to progress skiing, flirting with limits to live in a world without any.

The ski boom was happening and during the eighties Falls Creek was the place to be for many aspiring skiers. A lot of the mountain staff returned each year, with a variety of fabled characters, and they loved Team Red. Eric knew everyone, singing in the new era of freestyle with his no-rules-all-fun approach to life.

With a lot of hustling and hard work Team Red managed to gain greater sponsorships for skis, boots, clothes, eyewear and lift tickets, as well as sundries from local establishments, as their promotional power grew. These would serve as bonuses to ski more and work less, or to direct funding for competition fees and travel. Everyone was behind them with *'I support Team Red'* bumper stickers all over the Falls Creek car park.

The companies they were involved with received immense marketing benefit for their product association with world-class skiers. Everyone wanted their gear. While Team Red didn't quite figure out how to get paid for this, they certainly paved the way for modern alpine sports sponsorships.

Since the beginning, Bob Hymans wanted Eric to play his game in skiing by coaching younger skiers like Katie and Mark Steven. Bob was a close friend to John and Jean Steven, who built Pretty Valley Lodge, and Eric had skied with Katie a lot when she was on winter school holidays. Mark did his own thing and that's why they nicknamed him *The Professor*. Mark truly was a professor of skiing, studying every aspect, he had the style, he had the technique, he had everything and didn't need anybody.

If somebody told Eric about a *shit hot* skier, he was always sceptical with the exception of Mark Steven and Steve Lee, who were perfect skiers in his eyes. Steve had a lot of strength while Mark was more naturally gifted. What was great about Steve Lee was he loved to follow along and represent Falls Creek - he absolutely loved it! They all travelled together to competitions and these Falls Creek natives always stood out and did well.

For Eric and Lynne it felt righteously uplifting to see Team Red sporting fresh clothes, equipment and benefits, in exchange for on-mountain promotion. Showing off was their way of selling the dream. They were recognised when skiing, in person, photos, newspapers, magazines and brochures with sponsor logos on display.

Eric reckoned Team Red sponsors got their money's worth. 'No one was ever paid for modelling or movies,' he said, let alone sponsorship retainers or sales commissions like we hear about pro skiers getting today. If they sold an old pair of skis for pocket money that was the closest they got to sponsor income. It took a lot of figuring out and personal sacrifice to make it work. Frustrating negotiations obtained meagre support, yet there was no blueprint to what they were doing either. They were ski bums, not business or marketing graduates.

Before doing movies and being somewhat of a ski-clothing model, Eric specifically loved posing for action photos. If a photographer asked, 'Do you think you could jump off that rock?' Eric's retort would be, 'Can you take a good photo?' If they said yes he'd jump! It didn't matter so much how he landed as long as the photo came out good. Team Red were ski buddies, experimenting with form and function to push each other to greater thrills.

It just so happened that they attracted more people to the mountains and into Freestyle simply by sharing their love for what they were doing. Filming and photos were about art, not money, and an excuse to try new things and ski different places. To explore distant peaks and improve the technique it takes to experience every aspect. Healthy egos earned them fame and fortune (not remuneration), which expanded their opportunities.

Many attest to Eric having the flare that brought Team Red to life, he was a truly exotic personality.

Whether it was skis, skate, or a Ducati mixed with a mountain road - it was every bit thrill-seeking fun. Dropping a burly bump line on the Summit, skateboarding down the High Plains road, around blind corners not caring if cars were coming up, or riding bikes full speed (Falls Creek to Mount Beauty in seventeen minutes flat). Eric lived a fast paced life as a classic freestyle character. Which might sound like rock star living, but it wasn't easy because there was always a scarcity of money. Sacrifices had to be made to keep the lifestyle going. From all reports Bob Hymans didn't have a red carpet for his son, to the contrary he often treated Eric with utter contempt.

The endless-winter bug was taking hold and a growing number of Falls Creek skiers started following winter to Europe, specifically to Verbier in Switzerland, before it became a popular destination. Everyone in that group was working long hours, during and between seasons, to get over there. Some pulling tricks and scams to make it happen. Then banding together as a way to land a roof over their heads on the other side of the world. There are classic tales of fifteen people living on top of each other, as some accommodation became the go-to places for friends jumping on the freedom train. Scoring food to live, season passes to ride, and booze or drugs to party, were the only other objectives.

To tease collective normality, this new breed was flaunting the practice of liberty. Stepping outside the traditional social moulds of the nine to five grind.

Lynne Grosse. Bill Bachman photo

Team Red cover, Eric Hymans Summit Masters GC, Tracy Lee and Katie Steven.

Marriage; assets; family; retirement - were not on the radar. Live fast die young was closer to the mark. Girls flashed their boobs in public to break free of religious dogma. Anything to get high was open slather. Freeriders went against the grain to show off their form through skiing, surfing, riding bikes, on skateboards, in the air. Creating the means to make it all happen in spite of what society thought. It was a constant practice of challenging and overcoming fear to see what lay on the other side.

With Eric as an unofficial captain/coach, the whole freestyle ski posse was part of that freeride movement - trying new stuff, jumping off things, being crazy in the eyes of conservative people. Back in the seventies these forerunners of freestyle went to the absolute extreme end of the spectrum. Then were often reprimanded and squashed.

Eric's not sure of the proper way to explain events because he never formally studied the English language. That's probably why he swears a lot, from learning his raw Aussie lingo at Falls Creek. Forty something years later he still felt things were too controlled in the modern world. 'Where's the freedom? It doesn't matter what people are into as long as they are happy doing it,' and have respect for those around them. Eric spoke of no disrespect toward what other people do or where they have come from. He challenged the ones who judge, live in fear, or try to control situations. To some he was a bad boy because he didn't follow rules but to others he has been a liberator of the freestyle dream.

Eric demonstrated his level of freedom on skis sharing a story about Yogi at Falls Creek. Yogi was widely known for ski boot fitting at Moegel's Ski Mart, specifically the Lange brand, and used to supply Eric's sponsored gear. Yogi recommended Eric wear a smaller size ski boot. Eric told him to forget it because he felt comfortable in his size. He didn't want tight boots that hurt his feet skiing all day, every day, most of the year. Eric liked to be able to spread his toes and really press with the whole area of his feet to feel the ski arc through each turn. He didn't want everything to be compressed and restricted. He wanted to be free - 'Hey, that's why they called it freestyle!'

For a long time Eric lived in his ski boots. Always playing freestyle skiing games meant he stood with bent knees. He couldn't stand straight like normal people.

He liked to reminisce about the times he got up everyday and put his ski boots on straight out of bed. Clanking through the Man kitchen to do food ordering and all that before going onto the hill. It was a way to make the boots warm and comfortable. Then he could just go click click and be skiing. When the snow started getting slushy in the afternoon and heavy to ski, it was a sign for him to head back to the kitchen and prepare for dinner service. If the skiing was epic he wouldn't have time to take his boots off for work. Squeezing in one more run he often stayed in his boots till bedtime because he was most comfortable wearing ski boots. He wore those boots for such a large part of his life. It felt weird if he wasn't in them.

During the autumn of '83 Lynne and Eric, both then Australian champions, managed to score individual sponsorship for Dynamic skis and Look bindings. It was a promising step. Eric revisited his dream of becoming a ski tester, working on new performance designs. The tricky bit was figuring out how to get paid professionally. It was great to have free skis but they couldn't eat them or live in them. Dreams of formal careers in skiing were righteous but the ski market in Australia was small. They would have to make the ski industry rich before they would get paid for what they loved.

On the first snow of that year, Eric snagged his knee on a rock during a high-speed turn, which ended with him in plaster and off the slopes for most of the season. He was devastated, hoping to please his sponsors by winning another title. Suddenly he wasn't invincible and like anyone who has sustained an injury, questions started popping up about what was happening. Would he be back? The funny thing is that Eric was the type of guy who would reply 'fuck that!' to his own thoughts. He actually preferred it when he wasn't thinking at all. The world around him was changing and the answers as to why can be hard to find if you're not looking for them. Especially when someone is constantly accusing you of being unworthy of your family name or a failure for getting injured.

That season there were three freestyle events in the country at Selwyn Snowfields, Mount Buller, and Guthega. Eric and Lynne both encouraged Team Red to perform.

Peter Williams scored the win at Selwyn and placed third at the Abom Mount Buller. Mark Steven scored the Abom win. Then Team Red backed it up with Mark winning the Range Rover Mogul Championships at Guthega, alongside sister Katie who took out the women's championship.

Eric came off the sidelines to compete for the championship as well. After being out of plaster for ten days he loosened one binding to protect his knee. While doing a twister-twister-spread aerial manoeuvre over the first jump, his loose ski came off and he punched the rest of his run with only one ski. Placing seventh. Unfortunately Pete blew his knee at Guthega but the Falls Creek natives were dominating.

Collectively Team Red knew they had to rally support and develop a mogul competition at home, to showcase where all the progression was happening. Falls Creek skiing was the pride of the Australian ski industry and its Summit bumps would become a proving ground for the best of the best.

With no comp results due to his injury, Eric's sponsor sent him an invoice to pay the price of his free skis and bindings. This was a dire insult, as he was promoting their products when he hurt himself. Eric was already socialising more than usual from being off the snow. Something in the shadows was about to tip the scales, and dramatically affect his path as a ski champion. All of this was heavily influenced by his past, so to understand what made Eric tick we need to go back to his childhood.

Original chairlift at Falls Creek, built by Bob Hymans 1957

FALLS CREEK

Eric Hymans was born in 1957. The same year his father, Bob Hymans, built the first chair lift in Australia, possibly the Southern Hemisphere. Falls Creek has always been Eric's spiritual home.

He is far from being a rich man by any means but legend has it that the Hymans blood came from affluent Jewish stock. Three generations of insurance salesmen in Holland built respectable family standings. Eric's great grandfather ran a commercial shipping business and started insuring valuable goods between Rotterdam and Jakarta, back when nobody else would do it due to fear of pirates and navigation. An adventurous business legacy was built from this balls-to-the-wall approach, so wealth became associated with the Hymans name.

Eric's father Bob grew up ice skating and skiing across Europe, in a well-to-do environment, and was expected to take the family insurance legacy into the next generation. When the Second World War set in, the Hymans' fled to Indonesia where their family had acquired land through Dutch settlement. Bob started work for the merchant marine and in 1940 courageously joined a top secret intelligence vessel heading into the dangerous waters of the southern seas.

On the first day Japan joined the war, his ship was dramatically torpedoed and sank in Asian waters. Along with only one other survivor, he clung to debris and drifted for days until finally being picked up. Tragically their saviours were the enemy. As a seventeen-year-old boy Bob ended up a prisoner of war for five years with the Japanese. Slaving on supply routes, including Burma bridge over the river Kwai 1943. Knee deep in the blood, sweat and fears of all the things we hear about in the history of that era.

Bob Hymans only ever told Eric of his darkest experiences in that hellhole. How they were chained to the train carriages at night and jungle rats would attack their feet. One of the life long traumas these events created was said to make Bob violently try to kick anyone to death if they dared walk past his bed at night. The prisoners would eat the rats they killed and scavenge for anything to supplement their minuscule rice rations. Elephants were used for the heavy lifting. When one of them died the prisoners would be fed rotten meat after their captors had feasted.

Being the youngest POW in camp did gift Bob one special privilege: to be an old magician's assistant as he entertained the Japanese guards in their tents. The magician and his apprentice did tricks like making eggs vanish into thin air, and were received with applause and laughter. Toying with the heartstrings of the enemy to ease hardships was a devilishly clever survival tactic. A death-defying black market was formed to share the egg protein and one that flourished for the length of their imprisonment.

Bob's youthful imagination also helped him excel at the creative art of telling stories to his slave community. With inventiveness and distraction people can survive anything. Bob would grow to not only design and build things from nothing, but also be admired as an illustrious storyteller who captivated his audiences for the duration of his life.

When the war ended the POWs exited through Thailand, Bali and then onto Darwin, to fully regain their health before the long journey back to Europe. Their skin and bones from malnutrition were gradually filled with the love of beautiful hearts and communities. Bob would be forever grateful to good-natured people. That's when he fell in love with the lucky country and was instantly attracted to the Australian spirit.

He returned home to Holland with a dream of emigrating to the great southern land and to his family's disappointment decided not to take over the Hymans insurance business. Bob wanted to start his own legacy. While waiting for travel papers, he grabbed his skis and set out across post war Europe to explore the Alps. Those planks under his feet set him free. He loved being above the snowline, sliding down a mountain and teaching people how to ski. Fireside entertaining a big part of the attraction.

When the immigration gates opened, Bob flew first class to Melbourne. Once settled, he was recruited to play ice hockey after showing form at one of the rinks. During winter his team would take outings to Mount Donna Buang.

It was there that Bob discovered this country had snow. He was immediately excited to get back on the skis, with all their magical feelings that take one away from the troubles of life. He dreamt of taking on skiing Down Under and hit the trail toward snow-covered mountains.

Speaking fluent Dutch, English and German, with a bit of Japanese, Bob was hired by a French company that did hydro dam engineering. As a shop steward he helped communication between immigrant workers. In 1948 he ended up in North East Victoria. High above the Kiewa Valley in a little camp called Horseshoe Creek, so named after the boggy alpine marshes that would steal the shoes off horses. Bob worked on the Pretty Valley and Rocky Valley projects as they surveyed the Hydro Electric requirements.

In wintertime when it snowed, immigrants like Bob Hymans started skiing there. Bob went on to build a chalet called Four Seasons as the camp turned to a village. His dreams of life after completion of the hydro scheme, brought about a ski village that later became Falls Creek, so known for its cascading water.

Bob's mission was to share the thrill of sliding down a mountain with all these sunburnt Aussies and European refugees. Along with the likes of Tony and Skippy St.Elmo-Beveridge, who set up the first drag lift and ski lessons, Bob taught skiing to anyone who wanted to learn. He then went about building a guesthouse called Grand Coeur, which means Big Heart, for more people to stay on-mountain while learning to ski.

In time he set his sights on installing a chairlift, like the ones he had ridden in France. Travelling back to Europe to research such a development. Bob Hymans would be one of the first to fully commercialise skiing in Australia.

While shopping for chairlift parts in Europe, Bob fell in love with a beautiful Belgium girl, Mireille, at a ski area in the French Alps called Meribel. A lot of Europeans had suffered from the war and they shared this connection. Both had big hearts. Bob and Mireille were married in under six weeks and by the winter of '54 they were living together in the Australian Alps. In between birthing three children Mireille cooked meals, did laundry and entertained guests in Grand Coeur while Bob taught skiing, attended ski patrol and was one of the original mountain hosts throughout winter. They were the charm of snow skiing in Australia, with their European heritage, and trekked all over the high country on their skis - Spion Cope, Nelse, Mackay, Feathertop and Mount Bogong.

During summertime, Bob managed the design and construction of that first Australian chairlift. Which was engineered from scratch and assembled with second hand parts shipped from Europe. Once operational it was privately run by Bob, who would close it down for lunch to sit with his guests in the Lodge. The chair lift didn't have any safety switches so it had to be constantly monitored. This led to its eventual decommissioning when the Department of Labour and Industry declared it unsafe, just a few seasons after it had opened.

Mireille and Bob Hymans 1957

Around the same time, Bernhard Plohberger established the first Falls Creek skischool with Bill Bridgeford. These were the pioneering days of Falls Creek and Australian skiing as a whole.

Eric shared a story about Albert Costa (father of the famous bump brothers Paul, Adrian, Simon and Tom) coming to Falls as a nineteen year old Italian boy dressed in a suit and tie. After enquiring about snow work at the original Auski shop on Hardware Lane in Melbourne, Albert travelled to North East Victoria for a job at Mount Hotham. When that fell through, a bus driver mentioned a Dutch guy at Falls Creek was hiring on a new chairlift project. Albert caught a ski bus to Falls and met Bob Hymans on arrival. Initially, Bob didn't want anything to do with Albert because they didn't know each other. Then when Albert mentioned being let down on the Hotham job, Bob changed his tune. Bob was all about helping people who had been hard done by or struck with bad luck. So he threw Albert a shovel to dig a hole. Albert removed his dress coat and demonstrated his worth wearing a suit and tie. That night Albert moved into Grand Coeur and began his life at Falls Creek. Eric's mum called him Alberto and always let out a chuckle whenever she shared that story.

Another notable character of Falls Creek's early history is Orest Frueauf, who Frueauf Village is named after. One night Ore trudged through drifting boot deep snow to Eric's father's lodge, he saw Eric's mother cooking through the kitchen window, then went in to ask for a job.

That was Ore's beginning on the hill. Bob was a classic village backbone, who played a pivotal role in establishing Falls Creek as a magical ski destination. They named a run *Grand Coeur* after Bob. Which snaked the fall line near the original chairlift, between where the Gully lift and International poma were later installed. The run was misspelt *Grand Couer* during subsequent sign upgrades which the Hymans family found annoyingly humorous.

Bob was well known for having a big heart but was also somewhat of a hard case, not unusual for many war-affected pioneers. Talk of children being scared of him, being a recluse, or treating people harshly during those times, makes one wonder about the hardships Bob must have faced during his life. In any case Bob Hymans was all about skiing.

Bob was a dedicated ski instructor in the beginning. When there wasn't enough work at Falls he would teach in the morning. Then cross country ski thirty kilometres over the high plains to Shannonvale, where skiing had also started near the Blue Duck Inn, and teach over there in the afternoon. He would stay overnight entertaining his students then teach them again in the morning. After lunch he'd cross country ski back to Falls Creek. Bob made this trek once or twice a week.

Through the fifties, sixties and seventies Bob Hymans was one of the integral luminaries who brought Australian skiing to life. He bounced back and forth to Europe for Northern winter missions to teach skiing, chase powder snow and research new trends and technology.

Assisting the development of infrastructure that gradually turned Falls Creek into one of the great ski resorts down under. Bob was a well respected adviser. A sought after advocate of mountain life and endless winters.

Bob got people addicted to skiing by showing them how to fall in love with snow. A notable student of his was Kerry Packer, one of Australia's most successful businessmen, who ended up investing in his love of skiing by buying Perisher Valley ski resort in New South Wales. A lot of generational skiers paid homage to Bob Hymans.

Eric's spirit story is fascinating because he was conceived at Falls Creek. Just before he was born, Mireille went back to Belgium to visit her family. Then Eric popped out in Knokke-le-Zoute, a town on the Belgium coast. She returned to Falls six months later and introduced her young whippersnapper to skiing as soon as he could walk. Eric's two older sisters were also conceived at Falls and then born in Sydney, where proper maternity hospitals were available. All of them called Falls Creek their home.

The Hymans kept their family matters private. However, Eric recounted whispers from people who knew his mother and father when they were together, suggesting indiscretion. Distasteful feuds are usually birthed from a lack of trust and Mireille was one of the most beautiful women Australian men had ever seen. During Eric's infancy, rumours circulated to fuel Bob's torment. People would say, 'Eric looked more like a Fox than Bob,' hinting foul play from an engineer who worked on the mountain called Fox.

Such scenarios were impossible because Mireille was a kind, faithful and loving lady, but rumours can do strange things.

One can only imagine how hard it was for women back in those days. It got to the point when Mireille must have decided it was best to give Bob some space, only five or so years after they had married.

Legend has it that Eric's mum tried a couple of times to leave but wives were owned by their husbands back then. Legally she didn't have a leg to stand on. Mireille couldn't travel without Bob's permission. Local friends, who disagreed with Bob's behaviour, devised a plan for Mireille to escape. They solicited the support of a lady in the Belgian consulate in Sydney and managed to forge Bob's signature on the necessary travel documentation. Without Bob's approval Mireille returned to Belgium with her children when Eric was two years of age. Eric grew up in Brussels with his mum and sisters. Over the years, acquaintances discounted Bob in regard to his style of womanising. Becoming a recluse may well have been how Bob disengaged from communal bullshit.

In 1961 the Grand Coeur Lodge burned to the ground from a boiler room fire. Seventy guests fled into a cold and snowy night as the flames took hold. There was little forethought about safety regulations in the fifties. Not long after, the Summit and Village T-bars where installed at Falls Creek by Bill Bridgeford. Along with Eric's mum leaving his father, we are left wondering about the trials and tribulations that surrounded the Hymans family during those times.

Subsequently, Eric would not see his dad again before he was eight years old. After Bob was reunited with his children and started taking them skiing when he was in Europe.

In 1966 Bob partly inherited his elder sister's cottage in the South of France after she was buried by an avalanche at La Foux D'allos in the Alps and died. The family thinks it was from off-piste skiing, but Eric claimed Bob always told the story about how his sister (Eric's aunt) just pulled up in the car park, got out of her VW beetle and a roof avalanche came off a building and buried her against the car. Eric shook his head at that story, 'Not even skiing… at least if you're skiing there's a reason.'

Bob Hymans returned to Europe for his sister's funeral and then tracked down his children. The first time Eric realised he had a dad was when Bob turned up at their camp on the Belgium coast and declared he was their father. Bob couldn't even speak French properly. In agreeance with his sisters, they told the camp principal that they didn't know who this man was. It was another year before Eric saw his dad again, most likely due to legal procedure between parents. After that, Bob would pick his kids up to go skiing, or meet them at a train station in France, during school holidays.

An interesting thing was that Bob always insisted his kids call him 'Uncle Bob', because it was easier to meet women if he wasn't a father. Social stature was a big deal in those days and keeping up appearances was the done thing in Europe. Eric hated that part of his dad but there was love.

Bob was a grand storyteller who convinced a lot of people with make-believe and always had a yarn to share. Often his tales were perceived as fanciful but Eric hung off every word his father spoke. Everything had to be Bob's way.

Bob based himself at his sister's cottage each European winter when he was travelling for ski business or needed a getaway. He had been forging connections with other ski families who were starting ski lifts because that's what he had done at Falls Creek. When Eric skied with Bob they were always with people who were really into skiing. Eric's best flashbacks from his primary years were out skiing the Alps with his dad. He remembered bits of Austria, France and Switzerland. The clear picture given was everything being about skiing. Bob took all the kids on trips but Eric never knew what his sisters where doing while he was skiing. Sliding down a mountain on those two planks were the focal point of Eric's attention.

Bob was a traditional skier who loved ski racing, being super competitive he pushed Eric's abilities. Bob continually pestered Eric about living up to the Hymans' name in everything he did. If Eric didn't do things perfectly, Bob would get angry and claim they were not related at all. This behaviour lit a competitive fire inside the boy and by the time Eric was thirteen he started beating Bob at dual slalom. After that Bob stopped racing Eric altogether.

Bob and Eric Hymans in Holland during the late sixties.

Brigitte, Eric, Chantal and Mireille outside Four Seasons 1959

Chantal, Bob, Brigitte and Eric on a ski trip in La Plagne 1969

Eric Hymans in Brussels 1968

GROWING UP

During the early sixties, Mireille settled back with her parents near Brussels. As a mother of three without a husband, she may well have felt ostracized. Sadly, Eric's grandfather got sick shortly after and died of cancer. He had been a prisoner of war with the Germans and the torment was considered a contributing factor. Many families struggled after the Second World War.

Mireille found a job in Brussels doing paperwork at a hotel. Long hours meant Eric only saw her on the weekends. To ease the burden on their grandmother, Mireille enrolled her children in a *laïc* boarding school in Brussels called *école Plein-Air*. Eric's mum spoke fluent English and French so her skills were in demand. She got busy with a career. After some time in the hotel office Mireille moved up in the world and worked as a secretary for big companies such as IBM. Brussels was a strategic business hub in Europe, with lots of international corporations setting up offices there. The more she worked the more her children learned to look after themselves.

During holidays they attended extracurricular camps to keep them occupied. Mireille visited on weekends and Eric's eldest sister Brigitte looked out for her younger siblings inbetween. Forced to self-manage from a young age, the Hymans kids became more comfortable being away from adults. Eric felt essentially bought up by his two sisters and would spend his latter childhood with no parents around at all. Subsequently his personality evolved with an incredible amount of self-determination.

One of the camps Eric attended on the coast of Belgium, allowed the boys to roam into sand dunes and play games around deserted war bunkers that overlooked the ocean. He learnt to catch fish and prawns with the moving tides. Becoming one of the few boys permitted to help in the camp kitchen when his crew delivered their catch. Eric was good with animals and also earned the special privilege of feeding the very hairy Belgium Bouvier guard dogs, before all the kids went to bed.

The main guy that looked after the boys was an ex-para-commando who lectured them on how to survive like freedom fighters. Depending on their skill level, they'd be awarded summit stripes, which were simply painted lines on the brims of their green berets. They were taught how to climb through life to the peak of their potential. A highlight for Eric was his group building a four-sided high tower to scramble up. Each side increased in difficulty, with one side overhanging for abseiling full speed back to the bottom.

The boys also collected different motorcycle parts and learned how to build a bike from pieces. They practiced welding to hand make the frames from scratch. Then they'd go to meetings and race their bikes. Eric loved going fast and was considered the daredevil of his crew.

When they crossed paths with more formal boy-scout groups, they'd haggle over their outfits and badges. Eric's gang lived like a little Rambo squad with dirty faces and camouflage clothes. Challenging all their differences like young boys do. He loved those days and is glad with how he grew up. The impact of being thrust into such an early independence became both his strength and his weakness.

Over time Eric figured out how to do whatever he wanted. As one can imagine things got pretty wild by the time he became a teenager. Eric hated man-made rules and authority and yet deeply respected the laws of nature. Excelling at individual pursuits like climbing, horse riding and obstacle courses, he developed a knack for motivating other kids to find their own power and felt proud of who he was.

During the end of primary school Eric was sent to *Collège du Leman* Switzerland, a prestigious educational institution where the offspring of royalty and the famously rich were moulded. Part of him didn't fit in. He was always having trouble concentrating and seemed to be oblivious to authority. Eric returned to Brussels a year later and he figured his parents couldn't afford to keep him there.

Attending the *Lycée Français de Bruxelles*, Eric continued his wayward concentration in the education system. Inside the perimeter of this school was considered French territory and subsequently the Belgium police were not allowed to enter. Boys joked about evading the establishment and role-played life outside society.

By high school Eric occupied a different world in his mind from those around him. He became very creative. Making tie dye t-shirts and little trinkets, like dog collars, with leather from materials that a cobbler was throwing away. It was fun and a long way from family life. The summer of love had arrived and change was in the air.

Once Eric was a teenager, the standard of boarding houses across Europe was now frequently being challenged. There came a point when all the live-in students he was with united to protest about how their accommodation master was treating them. This rebellion resulted in the closure of his boarding house a year or two into high school.

Consequently Mireille made a special arrangement with Eric's original primary school boarding house, at *école Plein-Air*, to make exception for her kids to stay somewhere familiar. Living with younger primary kids while in high school was not ideal. They didn't appreciate being away from their own age group. One day the three of them walked out and marched back to their mum's house, demanding that they stay with her. Eric was old enough to catch a tramway to school by himself. No more boarding houses. The first time back at home, since living with their grandmother, felt like a dream and they rejoiced in the feeling of pure freedom!

Eric's mum lived in a two-bedroom apartment and the kids shared one room. Eric learned how to entertain himself after his sisters started going through puberty.

Most housing blocks in Brussels had a maiden room on the top floor for a caretaker or visitors. The one in their block was mostly vacant. Eric used that room as his own little palace to escape a surplus of female energy.

When Eric was thirteen his mum took him to spy on her boyfriend at the time because she had a feeling the guy was cheating on her. Sure enough it was true and her distress broke Eric's heart. Shattering it completely, the police arrived at their apartment after his mum was found unconscious in her car. Surrounded by medication, pills or something that ended with her at hospital in a coma. They believed it was a suicide attempt.

Social security was called to take the kids away. Then Brigitte rang the director of their school and he kindly took them in. Turmoil. Grief. Guilt. Maybe it was all his fault? Eric hated thinking his mum didn't want him around. Adults in general were rarely happy with his short attention span. It was too much for a young boy to fathom and Eric's world flipped.

Three months later Bob stepped in to help, once he was back in Europe. Taking Eric to a boarding school in the South of France near the beautiful town of Saint Paul de Vence. It was perfect to go skiing with Bob every weekend during the European snow of '70/'71. Whenever they weren't skiing Eric lived in oppressive hell. Forced to do schoolwork all the time, when his mind simply couldn't focus on textbooks for very long, he felt like a slave. After the winter finished Eric had to sit on a beach to study.

While his father was busy chatting to all the beautiful women who were sunbaking. After Eric returned to Brussels for the holidays he told his mum he couldn't go back.

Things were now different at home and he returned to boarding school at *L'Athénée de Forest* of Brussels. The focus there was on scientific study. Eric was good with animals, maybe he would become a vet?

The teenager was increasingly chastised because he couldn't sit still. Then he was caught taking the chains off toilet flush mechanisms. Eric had been making key rings to sell for pocket money. A young survival entrepreneur was improvising available opportunity. The teachers called it stealing. Eric was expelled.

Bob had rented a studio apartment for Eric's sisters, in the same block as their mum, as they prepared for university. Eric moved in on their couch and expanded entrepreneurial endeavours. He recalled his mum being constantly dumbfounded at how he always had money. He was enrolled into a special school for troubled kids but in similar fashion to his exit from boarding school, he earned reprimands from teachers for this or that. He rarely interacted with his mother. Eric didn't go to school much after that. Rapidly becoming more of a street kid with a lounge to sleep on, than a schoolboy with a home. Rather than finishing traditional school, Eric learnt the rhythms of a concrete jungle in his own 'school of life'.

During winter in Brussels, Eric looked out his window and it would be beautiful, too beautiful to be in school.

He had one of those classic sledges that you sit on with big-scooped-steel-sliders and timber on top. Across the road there was a park with some hills so he'd go there to hike runs. Then he'd go back to the apartment and grab his ice skates, get on a pushbike and fifteen minutes away there was an ice rink. He'd go ice-skating all afternoon, then play ice hockey at night. Eric loved skating and got right into it. Sledges or ice-skating filled his days during wintertime. Whenever he went skating with his dad, Bob would always be pushing him over and acting real heavy, to make him a stronger skater. His world became a mishmash of fun times and authoritarian despair.

Summertime was spent roller-skating or riding motorbikes with other free spirited youth. Eric got good at taking any old bike parked near his apartment and always put it back when he came home. One time returning a scooter, its pregnant owner was in labour and panicking for the hospital. Eric didn't realise anyone needed it for emergency and felt ashamed.

Bob was coming to take the kids on holidays so the three of them spent two days feverishly cleaning their apartment, without ever being shown how to do it properly. They really wanted to impress their father and show him they were worthy of the Hymans' name. When Bob arrived the first thing he did was wipe his finger across the top of a doorsill, where he found accumulated dust. This set off an angry tantrum because 'it wasn't good enough' so there would be no holidays for the children that year.

Whenever any of the three kids spent time with Bob it would always end in argument and disappointment. They were both generously accommodated and utterly terrorised youngsters, depending on their father's mood.

Eric's fondest memories were suddenly finding himself at a mountain resort to go skiing. Gradually he started figuring out that with ice-skating he could go backwards, do spins and all the fun moves - why shouldn't he be able to do that on skis? So he started trying all that stuff even though the equipment was not made for it back in those days. Using long two metre minimum planks, with no kick tails or side cut, he worked out how to do it.

Eric emphasised the importance of equal weight distribution through body position on skis that counted the most when doing tricks. Like a coach he confirmed that your belly button is a centre of gravity and everything pivots around that point. Whether it's on skis or skates, sleds or whatever, the whole game is played around central balance - you always got to be in that zone. Eric became addicted to skiing. Finding it so frustrating to go back to the lowlands and wait around till the next time he was able to get on a mountain again.

Bob didn't come back to visit one time and instead he hired a little hotel cottage in Saint Tropez for his kids' summer vacation. It had three single beds in it but two friends joined them. They pushed the beds together and five of them slept tip to toe. Saint Tropez was a ritzy holiday destination on the Mediterranean Sea.

A place where women sunbaked topless on the beach and many got fully naked. All these beautiful bodies evoked pubescent erections. It wasn't uncommon to duck off into the sand dunes and masturbate for sexual release. Puberty doesn't have to be an awkward time of life.

While walking around a marina precinct the kids got invited onto a yacht to drink beer and smoke joints. After some time Brigitte came to Eric all freaked out. They were leaving because the guys down below were only talking to them for sex. Eric was intrigued about what all the fuss was about so he stayed. Heading below to check out the party, some older guys asked if he was still a virgin. After he confessed, four French chicks in their twenties gave him the grand introduction, while a camera rolled. When he got back to the holiday cottage at five am, his sisters gave him a lecture because they were worried sick. They loved their little brother. Eric lost his virginity near the end of his fourteenth trip around the sun. This was one of his initiations to a life of drug-induced sexuality.

In Brussels, his sisters' shoebox sized apartment had a little kitchen, lounge and bed all together with a small bathroom on the side. Both of them attended university and romanced some very liberating, open minded and experimental times. Their bible was a cult literary classic titled *Les Enfants Terribles* (The Terrible Children) by French writer Jean Cocteau, about orphans who lived alone with no parents. It struck a chord and Eric was proud to be one of the wild ones.

For a while his sisters rigged a skewer in their door in order for friends to let themselves into their apartment without a key. Their flat became essentially a halfway house or drop in zone. Eric was the lucky kid who didn't have grumpy parents around or evening curfews.

He came home late at night one time and his middle sister's boyfriend was shooting up drugs on the couch, which doubled as Eric's bed. He walked in and the guy was trying to find his vein and he couldn't do it so he asked Eric for help. Eric was only a kid and didn't know what 'the fuck' that was. He had never even seen a needle before. Drugs were not the focus with their crew but freedom certainly was - anti-establishment, young at heart, living without rules or authority, trying new things. Anything taboo was explored. Punk rock came into fashion.

When Eric was fifteen he ended up in hospital himself from ingesting 'twenty grams of hash'. He was helping one of the guys who dropped in to weigh up portions and was eating bits and pieces like chocolate. All of a sudden he was on his arse and could hardly talk. When the paramedics took him to hospital, he managed to mutter an excuse that he'd drank a bottle of whiskey. While in the treatment room, a block of hash fell out of Eric's pocket and the doctor figured out what was going on. After a day or two in hospital the doctor had a chat to Eric about what he knew and even returned the block of hash he'd found! It is no surprise Eric held that doctor in high regard. When he got home his mum asked where he had been for three days.

Only seeing her occasionally, Eric had not considered the possibility that his mum was looking out for him.

    Another hash story version came from a Falls Creek friend who met Eric's mum and sister in Verbier one year. He recalled them telling some funny stories about growing up in Brussels, but not the usual ones you hear from a mate's mum. Eric's sister nearly got busted with a sizable amount of hash and before the cops could stop the car they persuaded their boy to eat the evidence. Then laughed when Eric's stomach got pumped, how the doctor couldn't see that as normal. Eric denied any memory of that one but all this stuff was simply a part of his teenage life.

    During the sixties and seventies it appears that drugs were everywhere, it was what everyone did. Europeans could smoke in aeroplanes, on trains and at restaurant tables. Bars sold alcohol on every corner and toilets were called powder rooms where people put stuff up their noses. Eric didn't know any different and remembered weighing up bags of speed to share with his friends so they could have a little buzz together. That's just how the world operated in front of Eric's eyes.

    Eric was naturally inquisitive and would venture out, under age, to experience live music. His sisters were so pretty that everyone loved them. They could get their little brother into the university concert hall when punk bands played gigs. The bouncers or musicians were always cool with Eric hanging around, because all the boys were trying to pick up his sisters. Eric got looked after so well.

He did whatever he wanted, with thanks to his beautiful sisters. Getting away with anything was how he grew up. Eric held deep love and gratitude for what they did for him. If it wasn't for them he 'would have got bashed a lot' and in all likelihood ended up in youth detention.

Eric's uncle, on his mother's side, had a restaurant not far from their apartment so from a young age Eric used to hang around there quite a bit. Helping clean up, pour beers, serve wine, as well as learning to cook in the kitchen. Over a number of years Eric acquired a vast amount of knowledge about European hospitality. Having worked as a chef in various places from what he picked up in his uncle's restaurant. He's not a qualified chef because he never did culinary school, but Eric's been a head chef many times and was widely celebrated for his flavours. Ask anyone who has lived with Eric in skier haunts, or eaten out of kitchens he's laboured at, and they all say the same thing. 'That dude can cook!'

Once it was clear Eric wasn't going back to school, he started getting paid for cleaning work. His first pay was scurried straight to the music shop to buy vinyl records. Rolling Stones, Pink Floyd, Lou Reed, Velvet Underground, Frank Zappa. The music of the time was so righteous and real, all were standing up to the status quo and singing in freedom. He 'fucking loved it!' Quite organically Eric became a rebel rocker, seeing all these epic musicians live on stage as they toured through Brussels. Not to mention plenty of romancing at all the after parties

- Sympathy for the Devil and Dark Side of the Moon.

Weekends meant late night gatherings around their tiny urban apartment. One night an older guy, who had done time in jail for LSD related charges, did a prison style tattoo on Eric's arm with a needle taped to a pen. A freehand Rolling Stones tongue because Eric was their biggest fan. It took eight hours while a crazy party flowed around them. There was always something wild going on. Smoking. Drinking. Trying new things. Listening to loud rock music. Telling jokes and laughing hysterically.

Eric's respite from that world was whenever Bob picked him up to go skiing during the wintertime. He'd have to smarten up and get really proper, to please Bob's high expectations of the Hymans clan. When everything was cool they would hit the road to go skiing and ice-skating in the heart of the Alps - La Plagne, Chamonix and Verbier.

Eric remembered when Lange first released plastic boots in 1966, compared to the leather ones. It was a revolution! By the late sixties everyone was making them. He'll never forget the day that Bob and Eric finally got to try these new plastic ski boots. Both of them ended up at the medical centre in the afternoon with knee injuries. What a laugh. They couldn't use their ankles any more as it was all done with the knees. Skiing was evolving and with plastic boots they needed to learn a totally different way of skiing. The stiffness dramatically improved edging power. Eric was fascinated with the whole progression from wooden skis all the way through to click on bindings.

Eric Hymans in Belgium 1974 - Jeep Novak photo

BIRTH OF FREESTYLE

Eric remembered the birth of freestyle spirit in the early seventies with fond recollection. Bob was a very, very orthodox skier, done by the rulebook. He was the only non-French invited to the French Ski School in Chamonix because he was respected around the world. When Bob saw Eric developing a more free-style in his skiing, he liked it because it was different. Bob had been skiing since a young age and when he saw something fresh he encouraged Eric to explore it. Away from the racecourse and into the bumps, they started calling it hot-dogging. All the hot skiers showed off to vie for top dog on the mountain, by skiing the best lines with style. This new way of skiing wasn't recognised and it provoked debate on a whole new realm to discover.

Everything was about pushing the boundaries and having the most fun. The best part being the clowning around. With father and son speaking a few different languages between them, they developed their own lingo nobody could understand. Essentially they became a two man private circus. Eric learnt to change words around for the fun of it. In French slang they called it *Verlan* and it became fashionable in the '80s and '90s, where people reversed the syllables of each word for a laugh.

It's a play with linguistics so that others can't understand what is being said. Unless they are connected to the greater spirit of freedom and can read communication energetically. Reversing letters and words became a bit of a verbal game in freestyle during the seventies. Later in music they called it hip-hop.

One time at breakfast on a ski trip, there were some women wearing overalls in full seventies fashion with straps around their boobs. Eric and Bob were carrying on like schoolboys talking about their tits in another language. They had such a laugh speaking their own lingo in different countries so nobody could understand them. Along with the new moves on skis, came the new cheeky attitude that revolved completely around fun and freedom. Exploring outside the box to connect with everything on a less verbal, more spiritual plane.

Before the European Union was formed there was a group of states called Benelux, which involved an open border agreement between Belgium, Netherlands and Luxembourg. As Eric became more absent minded while dreaming up freestyle, he was getting greater exposure to the drug scene and floating between cultures. Brussels was the melting pot where French heritage mixed with Dutch and there was a distinct smell of anti-establishment in the air. If Eric didn't find a suitable occupation he was going to end up in more serious trouble.

Mireille figured one way to get her son off the streets was to organise a job for him with the merchant marine.

Bob didn't like that idea, after his distressing time at sea, so Mireille suggested Eric go to Australia and work in his lodge at Falls Creek. She felt Eric needed a full-time father figure to properly develop into his manhood, even though she'd had issues with his dad.

Eric's friends in Brussels were saying, 'Fuck that's a long way,' which made him a little apprehensive. Bob was giving him heaps of grief about who he was becoming in the eyes of the old world. Hating Eric's tattoo due to all the persecuted Jews having tattoos in the war, but Eric loved it when they were skiing together. Skiing was Bob and Eric's connected passion. He looked at some maps that showed Falls Creek a long way away from any cities and wondered what life would be like in the middle of nowhere. Bob mentioned the children of doctors and lawyers, who took ski holidays at Falls, also smoked pot and listened to rock 'n' roll so Eric would make new friends easily. With his mum's strong encouragement, Eric accepted Bob's invitation to move Down Under.

Eric flew to Melbourne prior to the Australian winter of '75. Coming through customs he was detained for having a few grams of hash in his pocket and a bag of cannabis seeds stashed in his suitcase. It hadn't crossed his mind that would cause any trouble because marijuana was an acceptable barter where Bob was from in Holland. Anyone could buy the stuff in coffee shops and they had never been searched crossing borders before. Handcuffs, fingerprints, photos and a police car to the remand centre.

'Welcome to Australia Mr Hymans,' a smart-arse remarked.

Bob was pissed off. Legally charged with the potential of what each of those seeds could produce, Eric sat behind bars and thought about getting a few more prison tattoos for his father's distaste. The remand centre was adjacent to Her Majesty's Pentridge prison maximum-security lockup, where many wild outlaws of the day were sent when caught not following the rules. Eric breathed in stories of Ned Kelly and other famous Australian gangsters, who had been wrangled and hung inside the haunted walls of that place. It was a mix of guards using scare tactics and inmates glorifying criminals.

Eric began to think that Bob had left him in there to rot and wondered if he would ever be free. Obviously there was a bit of work done to have the charges dismissed and the boy out on a good behaviour bond. Bob later stirred Eric about the delay in bailing him out being a blessing for Eric's character. Bob had survived his time as a prisoner of war – for him, internment made a man stronger. Good or bad it became the crux of a love hate relationship between an absent father and an estranged son. Bob told Eric he wasn't good enough to hold the Hymans' name and therefore was in no way his biological son, a sentiment Bob increasingly repeated throughout Eric's life. Bob's distrust for people would fester from his war experiences. The worst part for Eric was that his father had money and there were always power plays when he tried to get his way.

Odilon and Eric, best friends forever, Brussels '74

Bob came to get Eric out of jail and stopped at a hotel in St Kilda, which was the red light district of Melbourne. He gave Eric twenty dollars to entertain himself while Bob visited some friends. Eric went out for pizza and then got talking to a girl in a bar, who ended up back at his hotel room for the night. Eric's thinking 'Australia isn't a bad place after all,' considering pizza and soft drinks cost less than ten dollars and he got laid without even trying.

In the morning the girl got up to leave and went through Eric's wallet taking his other ten dollars. Eric pretended to still be sleeping as she exited and didn't bother hassling her about the money, 'It was worth it for the sex.' Under Eric's skin his trust toward women, other than his sisters, would become increasingly elusive.

Eric arrived back to his spiritual home of Falls Creek fifteen or so years after he'd been whisked away to Europe as a two year old. One of the first people he met was a lift operator by the name of Jim Darby, who was fascinated with storytelling language and loved visiting Bob to hear all his classic tales. Eric didn't speak much English yet so Jim took him up to the Frying Pan to watch the latest Warren Miller ski film - *There Comes a Time*. Then they went skiing together and with Jim's help Eric started picking up some local lingo.

Falls Creek kids like Bob Irwin were always a bit frightened by old Bob Hymans, a real recluse, so it was a shock when this nouveau hippie turned up with a really strong accent, claiming to be the son of Bob.

Eric could cook, make his own Campari, but could he ski?? He had a style that was very typical of the freestylers of that era - part daredevil, part epileptic, with tons of impressive airtime in the bumps.

One afternoon in the Frying Pan, Hans Fischer and Bruiser confronted this young skinny guy, asking his origin? 'Belgian,' Eric pronounced. Hans grunted something and Bruiser said, 'Fuck knows where that is,' so they nicknamed him 'French Eric' and the moniker stuck. Hans was manager of Fryers at the time and when Eric came up to the bar with glassy eyes and ordered lemonade, he immediately pulled him up. 'Are you on the green? Listen here mate, we don't trust anyone who doesn't drink beer around here so you'd better pull ya head in.' Eric promptly changed his order to beer.

Unknowingly Eric's destiny was unfolding. During his first season at Falls he felt like a fish out of water. His skiing style took a lot more effort in the heavier snow and his manhood was constantly being challenged. The rough necks called him a poofter because he had earrings in his right ear, when 'real men' only wore them in their left. 'How strange,' Eric thought, 'Europeans decorate their right ear because that is where the ladies look when you're dancing with them.'

With a harsh Aussie culture surrounding him, Eric had to stand up and show what he was made of. Luckily, he had been unceremoniously groomed in the art of survival, hospitality and open mindedness, with roots deep in skiing.

Mixed with core strength from ice-skating, the street smarts of a wild boy, looks that made women weak at the knees, European charm, and his unique connection from being conceived right there in Falls Creek, Eric Hymans possessed all the ingredients to become a mover and a shaker.

Two planks under his feet became his power base and with serendipity on his side he got to ride them every day. His upbringing, with all the clashes against authority and the heartache from his parental separation, had been somewhat disempowering. Skiing would ultimately empower Eric and be something solid that nobody could take away from him. It only took Eric a year or two before his future form started showing, as the full flight of freestyle began to take shape and turn heads.

The balance skills gained from ice-skating and speed skills from motorbikes would consolidate a volatile ski repertoire. Over the next decade this helped turn Falls Creek into a freestyle hotspot for generations to come.

Eric had an epiphany one day sitting at the bottom of the Summit. Looking up and analysing the mountain he came to realise that there was so much to do with it, so many rocks and trees to play with! Nobody was skiing the lines Eric started visualising. These were the days when freestyle skiing was just starting and Eric naturally evolved into one of freestyle's pioneering forerunners. He had magically been sent to the right place at the right time, with his unique combination of experiences. The world was going to learn the name - Eric Hymans.

Steven Lee put things into perspective:

Our family goes a long way back with the Hymans, my mum and dad travelled Europe with Bob Hymans in the seventies and that's when they first met Eric. He was seventeen or eighteen and not in a great way, living from what I've been told pretty much on the streets of Brussels, with a nasty drug dependence. Bob got him out of there and brought him to Falls Creek, which likely saved his life. It was there skiing became his (main) drug!

While his party life continued, skiing was a big part of his life also, and through the sport he was happy and healthy. He did however remain a party animal! I could draw comparisons to Rolling Stone Keith Richards but no matter his state, Eric could get out and ski those summit bumps like a fucking demon! Perhaps that's why he proudly sports the famous Stones mouth emblem tattooed on his arm.

From a competitive perspective, he loved it, he loved being in the hunt, but also loved seeing his mates or teammates prosper. He was an integral part of building the legend of Falls Creek's freestyle gang, Team Red. At comps, while very competitive in his own right, was always super supportive, humble in victory or defeat, and bloody good fun to have around. From my generation he's one of the real characters of the Falls Creek community, and now he's bloody sixty! Perhaps his greatest achievement! On ya bro!

The 'Keith Richards' of freestyle skiing settled into Four Seasons Chalet as the new cook. His father might have been impressed by Eric's prowess in the kitchen but would never be one to acknowledge it. Bob had an interest in time and motion so if things weren't perfectly efficient someone would hear about it, and he was most critical of Eric.

A freestyler's different way of thinking on the mountain was also applicable in the kitchen and Eric played a part in influencing the direction of mountain cuisine from that point on. The food of the time was predominantly British and Eric brought into the mix his style of European, Moroccan, North African and Middle Eastern flavours to the dinner table.

The policy in Four Seasons was that you had to go skiing. A big cowbell was clanged every morning at breakfast time to get everyone up and out on the hill. If you weren't there to ski then you weren't welcome to stay. This attitude was relevant to how Eric's skiing developed. People came for the food and the stories as well as the downhill slide. Plus, Bob preferred guests smoked grass than drink booze because they would chill out and listen to his tales rather than get drunk and make a ruckus. An enlightened Dutch strategy.

Out of the kitchen Eric dived into construction, like his father had done, and built himself a private room in the attic space of the lodge. Lifting a roof area and installing a king size bed above the hot water services to keep warm, with a little lounge area and window.

Eric Hymans with Village T-bar in background. Falls Creek.

Finding mystique from the talk around town, he took in Bob's quarter century of local experience like a youthful sponge and expanded his knowledge of the Australian Alps.

    Most mountain staff on the hill shared cramped four-bunk rooms. Eric's pad was like a ski bum penthouse and that's how it was treated. Monika Plohberger described it like a sixties Hendrix palace with cool music and incense burning among other smells. Although, getting in and out of that place, up and down a steep tight ladder in various states of inebriation, was often an impossible dream for those less skilled. Eric was like a monkey doing it every day and when friends couldn't handle it, they would vomit out the window if they got too intoxicated, instead of trying to exit in time.

    The visitors were many, the parties went long, and the only true cure for a righteous hangover was time on the hill. This new ski bum party lifestyle pushed the envelope on what was physically possible. Like a punk rock song playing loud over a mosh, the band's musical instruments were their skis and Eric took on the job of lead vocals for freestyle. At first it wasn't easy but that didn't matter because Eric truly loved his world with no rules. Skiing without any limits. His old man used to tell him:

    Hang the expense just go for it. Rules or regulations do not apply. The only thing that really matters is what's in your mind. Once you know what you want to do you just go out there and do it. Find a way. You still want to be safe, and make sure you are, but if you get hurt along the way it's all part of the deal.

So Eric was into doing things differently and some people loved that. Freestyle really felt like a revolution and inherent during those times was a distinct feeling of change. Like in the sixties with women burning their bras, freestyle was all about liberation and finding greater freedom in life. It was an exciting period in skiing history. Being one of the first to be doing freestyle in Australia was like riding a wave of individuality for Eric.

Since then Eric has seen it grow from the search for what's fresh and new. It is a different way of thinking that makes it interesting and it's applicable to all aspects of living. Mathematics is a big thing in freestyle, from equipment to body positioning there is a whole science going on behind it. Eric became very fastidious about his equipment and his form, carrying around a pocket ski-tuning kit and tools to adjust things on the fly.

Teaching himself freestyle simply by adapting his ice-skating skills to skiing - one eighties, three sixties, using the outside edge as well as the inside edge. Trying anything and everything to increase the fun. Eric dreamed about how nice it would be to study these things at college and get kids interested in the body mechanics. His way of thinking didn't fit into the old system of education.

The grizzled guard in the ski school didn't like the way Eric Hymans skied because he didn't follow the rulebook on how to ski! They wanted to maintain the status quo but Eric saw their way of skiing as boring and out-of-date. He was a rebel.

Freestyle was underground and new, born from a universal shift happening at that point in the planet's history. One can imagine the snow scene during the seventies, like the surfing scene in those days, being full of alternative thrill seekers who were travelling and finding new waves and mountains, rejecting convention and seeking epic times.

Eric was definitely one of the alternative thrill seekers and rumours had spread about him being a jailbird, so he immediately gained a bad boy reputation. He was an outsider - the guy who doesn't live by the rules. Unbeknownst to Eric he started getting noticed on the hill, gradually showing up many a good skier of the day with his European form and freestyle mind. Simply by doing things differently, Eric became a bad boy on skis too. Out there, every day, in any weather, searching for an adrenaline rush. Not following any regimented traditions, while taking anyone along for the ride if they were interested. He was a game changer - THE game changer in Australia.

On the slalom course Eric started to use the outside edge of his inside ski to step up and out of each turn, when everyone else was just carving their inside edge of their outside or downhill ski. He was breaking convention but this put him in a better position for the next gate, making things faster and more fun. It was a weight transfer technique he developed from ice-skating and he won a few slalom races. When the bumps started being the place to ski, that's also what he did to put himself in the best line.

Some people you see jumping from the top of bumps to the top of the next bump being aggressive. Eric liked to flow between the bumps like water, smooth and fluid like. He was a dancer not a fighter. Which makes a massive difference in what people like to watch and how it feels to ski. This is one of the ways he tuned into the sweet spot on moguls to gain the most airtime. Doing things differently will always be the hallmark of great freestyle and that was Eric's speciality.

Eric's original Gitane Testi road bike with Motoreli Minareli engine. Brussels '74

LOCAL KNOWLEDGE

As soon as the snow melted, the thrill seeking continued and Eric turned his focus to riding bikes. Those who know the Bogong high plains around Falls Creek know it is a biker's paradise. From dirt enduro to road touring, motor or pedal, nowadays mountain biking, it's up there with some of the best places to ride on Earth. Before high country bike riding became so popular, there was the dream of biking and Eric was one of those dreamers.

Eric was exploring the area when it was mostly dirt roads around Falls. One summer out behind Rocky Valley dam, at the old quarry on Basalt Hill, the boys bustled the loose rocks around to build a racecourse for their dirt bikes. Bill the old copper comes along and asks what they were doing? Eric tells him they are making a place to ride their bikes, so as not to ride through all the bushes destroying nature. They had nothing to do up there in summer and wanted somewhere to have some motor-cross fun. The old copper goes, 'No worries Eric, go for it.' Bill knew Eric's old man and the boys were always trying to do the right thing. Eric's bike was unregistered and not road worthy but Bill was cool with that. Eric was a well-established rider and known to be very cluey with bike mechanics and performance tuning.

Like most wild boys, the opportunity to rev an engine was a high priority for Eric. His experience from building bikes in Belgium set him in motion. Having that power at his fingertips and agility between his legs was a special feeling. Totally addictive. It shared many physical and mental attributes to skiing that made him strong and focused in the moment. Once Eric got hold of a bike he'd ride it for hours, often all day long. He soon met other bike riders searching out the best circuits. Off the hill there was a motorbike track in Tawonga where crew haggled each other. A few people spoke of Eric taking some scary spills here and there but nothing that caused him serious injury. Always stoked when pinning it up the hill back to Falls.

Bob told the boys stories about building a little bridge across Pretty Valley dam, when he worked for the French company that managed the Hydro Scheme. How it allowed access out to some huts toward Mount Feathertop. Wild horses and black wallabies had been spotted along with wedge-tailed eagles. The more places his father spoke about the more Eric would explore. Far and wide he rode, getting to know the area like few others. It was his backyard. Through Bob's longstanding experience, Eric became part of the high country and fully embraced Falls Creek as his home.

He remembered people hiking in the mountains and they'd get lost. Police or the SES (State Emergency Service) would come to find Eric because he knew the land. Like an old aboriginal soul who had that sixth sense or inexplicable connection to see and hear and feel what others couldn't.

Of course he'd help get a group together because you can't go out searching alone. The cops would have 'all these wiz bang motorbikes registered or whatever' and Eric had his beaten up dirt bike, loud and unregistered. They'd go out in pairs with the police 4wd support carrying forty-four gallon drums of fuel. Everything was kosher and they'd invariably save the people. Mountain folk have a real sense of belonging and now Eric was one.

Eric has seen some big cats in the high country. Many have heard the urban myths of panthers or whatever escaping from a travelling circus and roaming the countryside. Well, Eric doesn't make those claims but he has seen some big feral cats a few times. Many wouldn't believe him but he swears it's true. Not saying tigers or pumas as such, but big enough to make your hair stand on end. One time near Strawberry Saddle he came around a corner on his dirt bike and surprised a small pack of them - cats as tall as his knees, making him fear they could jump up and knock his bike over. They didn't of course and scattered from the engine noise, but he's seen them. When an old mountain man tells stories like that, it does make one wonder.

Apart from riding around on bikes, the thrill seekers would build skateboards from bits and pieces. Then roll them down smooth sections of the sealed mountain road. Pushing fear hooting and hollering with wind in their hair. A car would tow them back up to where they had started. Not much to do in summer back then so they got creative.

One time, local crew built a ski jump out of metal to practice aerials. Skiers launched into the water of Rocky Valley Dam. They'd wear a wetsuit and use old boots and skis they no longer cared about. They didn't need the equipment to be precise. The thing that had to be precise was their body position. Not the ski boot or the ski as part of the apparel to get them into the air. It was body movements that had to be precise to achieve what they dreamt of doing, before landing in the water. These stories from Eric demonstrate the pathways his generation took to achieve new levels of form in freestyle.

During the winter of '77, the Falls Creek community built a jump beside Snowland Supermarket to hold a bit of a freestyle demonstration. With shallow snow it went over the road and into a pile of hay. Hundreds of bails of hay all fluffed up and called a hay jump. Every time an over-snow vehicle went past they'd be jumping over it. That's how they practiced freestyle back in the seventies.

I asked if any of his generation has ever taped up the edges of their skis to bounce on a trampoline for practice? Eric agreed it's a good idea but that sort of thing only came in once aerials entered the Olympics. After that, freestylers created specific Olympic training camps that incorporated advanced water jumps with air bubblers to break the surface tension. As well as foam pits in trampoline gyms. In the seventies they were just coming up with these ideas to take air awareness to the next level. He was again at the forefront.

Snow Crystal Inn, party house at Falls Creek.

Eric was continuously tuning his eye toward the best equipment. Increasing his knowledge about technology. He cast his mind back to when they invented ski stops. Look bindings were always well loved, but at the start they 'fucked up' by pointing the brakes forward under the toe. 'If you carved too hard past bushes or chunky snow they would grab and take you down.'

It happened to Eric once going full speed across the Summit at Falls Creek. He got told off so many times for going fast, timing the Village T-bar to fly across and down Gully for the longest run possible. This one time there was a cable just under the snow (an ironic remnant from Bob's original chair lift) and Eric's ski stop caught it. Taking him down so hard he blacked out and woke up fully winded. When he looked up there were people staring at him. The ski stop was all bent out like a trip hazard. He picked himself up, put his skis on his shoulder and walked out. Soon the binding design was changed to back brakes like they have on skis today.

When the lodge was closed during off-seasons (spring or autumn), Eric was employed at various times by Falls Creek Resort Management. Working on expansion of ski runs: out in the Maze; over at Lakeside; down Towers; Panorama; Wombats Ramble; The Last Hoot; and the Home Trails. Geoff Dyke worked on a crew with Eric and an old mate nicknamed Yoney. They would do brush cutting, lay straw for re-vegetation and dig drainage for snow retention. Constantly in hysterics with Eric.

One time Geoff was teasing an alpine funnel-web in it's hole, poking it with a stick, then all of a sudden the damn spider ran up his leg! He turned to Eric in distress and, without hesitation, Eric belted Geoff across his shin with a shovel and nearly broke his leg. Geoff still replays the speed of Eric's reaction in his mind and it's one of his favourite stories because Eric always meant well, but often didn't think of the consequences. Impulsive reactions were part of Eric's character.

Eric also worked on the original village sewage system, or poo-farm as some would call it. To coin a phrase he used to say, 'Falls Creek Treatment Plant - It might be shit to you, but it's bread and butter to us!' and those exact words ended up on their staff t-shirt. He is one of those guys who always loved to have a laugh.

Another time the Mount Beauty police sergeant was walking in Falls and bumped into Bob. The sergeant asked how Eric was doing and Bob mentioned he was just on his way to see the lads, as they must be having smoko by then. He invited the cop up to the flat. Eric was there as expected with his mate having tea and biscuits, with a joint turning the place into a Dutch oven. They're sitting there with an ounce of green on the table, and the next minute the front door opened and it was Bob with the police officer behind him. He looked in and calmly announced, 'Eric, I think you better turn the fan on.' Eric was sitting in front of the bag of pot with the sergeant looking down at him. He casually put the joint down in the ashtray, still burning, then Bob and Eric together put on like nothing was out of the ordinary. 'Would you like a cup of tea mate? Or a soft drink? There is some soft drink in the fridge.' The policeman was either none the wiser or didn't bother letting on and it ended up all cool. Eric laughed hard at those memories.

Even though Eric didn't have a licence, he used to drive down the mountain to collect supplies on his father's instruction. Bob would say, 'If the cops pull you over just say nobody knows you have taken the car.' After a while Eric figured he needed to get a licence so he walked into the police station, when it was still on Lakeside Drive in Mount Beauty, and asked the sergeant at the time if he could get one. The police had seen him driving his father's car up and down the road for quite some time and were a little surprised. Old man Hymans didn't care about licences and permits and all that formal stuff.

The sergeant told Eric to come back the next day and conduct a learner's test. The following day Eric walked into the police station and there was a test on the table next to a learner's book. He went through the questions, checking all the answers in the book, and once he was finished the cop came over and said, 'No worries Eric, you got all the questions right. Come back with a car and we'll do a driving test.' Eric picked up the EH Holden he had driven off the hill, with a faulty parking brake, and did a bit of a drive around the block with that copper. Back at the station they gave him a licence for both bike and car on the spot.

BJ & Eric ruling foosball at the Frying Pan. Damien Pierce photo

That's how Eric got his licence many years after he started driving. Rules meant nothing to him but he had an acute sense of common courtesy.

Eric was involved in whatever was happening around the hill: Gatherings in the Frying Pan playing foosball (table soccer); Little dashes to Snow Crystal staff house for bongs; Late night after-parties in his illegally constructed attic room. There was a consistent flow of visitors from all over the country who loved French Eric's charisma. Many brought with them a regular supply of goodwill offerings to eat, drink, smoke or snort. The things that proceeded way outside the societal norms and rules are what made legends. Everyone wanted to be a legend and just hanging out with one was the next best thing. People always treated him like skiing royalty at Falls Creek. It was organic social growth without any instruction manual. They were unashamedly wild times.

When Mike Haid came to town from Canada he was told to go to the pub and meet a guy called Eric, 'He can ski, find what ya need and will show you around.' The local lads adopted this Canadian bump skier and he ended up hitching a ride to comps with Team Red. They nicknamed him Flash because he skied in motocross pants with a flash logo on the back.

For a good stint Eric became a host of sorts to the whole attraction of the High Country and growth of freestyle skiing, for an eclectic mix of people. Maybe even more than Bob did within the ranks of orthodox skiing.

The legend of French Eric found a warm place in the hearts of common people, while at the same time being an enigma and danger to the pompous highbrow outside world.

Some crew called him a Chipmunk because he was good looking, he could ski and everything about him was mischievous. He was mysterious and exotic like his own type of animal, with a persona somewhat animated like a cartoon. It wasn't unheard of for women to notice Eric above all the other available men in social circles and fantasise about sex and glory. He boasted about never really having to put much effort into picking up girls. They would often just be waiting to walk home with him at the end of each night. A friend called Sasha, who was a good looking Eastern Block immigrant, started having contests with Eric about sleeping with girls. Like Austrian ski instructors, they were the flavour of the day.

One such girl was that gorgeous surfer chick by the name of Lynne Grosse and she would hold Eric's heart for some time. Lynne came to Falls Creek in '78 as an Australian female skateboard champion from Adelaide, who had grown up in gymnastics and surfing. The first time Eric saw her, he recognised something special in the way she moved effortlessly around her core, with a real sense of connection to motion. She took to skiing like a natural under Eric's wings, with his worldly charm, and immediately displayed the potential of a champion.

As 'the dark horse from down under', Lynne Grosse had won the 1976 World Skateboarding Championships.

At only fifteen, she was invited to compete at Magic Mountain in Los Angeles by Stacey Parelta and Russ Howl. Tom Sims, a skate and snowboard pioneer, had style and she sessioned with Tony Alva, Jay Adams and all the legends of the sport. The prestige of victory scored her a job featuring in a TV commercial. Lynne skated down a Hollywood hill with a cereal box in one hand and an American flag in the other. The director insisted she do it about twenty times until the cameraman was satisfied they got the shot. On the last take, her wheels found a pebble that launched her onto the asphalt. She broke her thumb along with road rash.

Fun California crew took her under their wings for a month, checking out skate spots and sharing medicine. Peer pressure and drug use went hand in hand. When she tried some it made her mind trip out and go all warped. The skate parties she hit with that crowd all turned into riots. TVs and furniture got thrown off balconies and into swimming pools. Police would come and everyone would run.

As part of the Golden Breed team, Lynne had saved up the money for her airfare to America by selling swag to other kids at school and doing fundraisers around her hometown of Seacliff. When she returned from her LA win, sponsors paid her expenses to tour Australian and New Zealand schools and shopping malls to promote skating! During that tour Lynne collided with a car on a busy city street and was out of action again. By the time she recovered the winter had ended her skateboard season. There were no indoor parks for kids back then.

Eric Hymans and Lynne Grosse, Les Chalet 1979

Some surfers from the Golden Breed family suggested Lynne check out the snow and a new craze called freestyle skiing. That's how Lynne ended up meeting Eric. When they weren't skiing they were always hunting out new ways and places to play. Now it seems like all that enthusiasm laid the foundation because it sparked major interest in the decades to follow. Skate parks and snow parks both came from that desire to chase the balance buzz.

The years that Lynne and Eric skied together became folklore. People ended up calling them the Sid and Nancy of skiing, like the bass player from the Sex Pistols and his girl, wild trailblazers with free spirit and fun-loving attitudes. Living on the edge like full punk rockers. Naturally, some people didn't like that Eric and Lynne were into doing drugs and partying as much as skiing.

After that first winter together, Eric took Lynne road tripping on his Honda CBS350 motorbike from Falls Creek to Phillip Island. Eric tried his hand at abalone diving with Gary Braid. Making three hundred dollars in a day with his biggest haul. Lynne worked at the local pub for three dollars fifty an hour. Beer only cost twenty cents a pint so life was doable. Lynne took Eric into the waves and tried to teach him surfing but Eric preferred to thrash his bike around the island's famous Grand Prix circuit. They stayed with ski friends, the Van Puttens, and were living how many dreamed of living - with no fear. Purely for the ride with all the fun and adrenaline that goes with it. Surviving hand to mouth each day at a time.

Adventuring from that summer holiday season, Eric and Lynne toured the whole length of the Great Ocean Road to Adelaide. Her guitar somehow strapped to the back with their tent and gear, easy-rider style. Continuing their quest for thrills. The bike broke down one time and Eric fixed it by rebuilding the carburettor in an overnight caravan they rented, leaving oil stains everywhere.

Arriving in Seacliff, Lynne's parents wouldn't let them sleep together under their roof because their daughter was seventeen and Eric was twenty. Instead, the kids pitched their tent in the backyard. Lynne showed Eric where she grew up and they went skateboarding. Rolling the banks of a velodrome. Going fast down concrete storm water drains. Surf styling the walls of a friend's empty swimming pool. Playing with gravity and riding transitions was such an adrenaline rush. In the history of skateboarding these were the brutal days of Dog Town and that free spirit wasn't confined to California, it was oozing out all over the world. Skating and freestyle were going crazy in the seventies.

When they left Adelaide Lynne picked up her pet cat and they made a little box for it next to her guitar on the back of the bike. In the spirit of indigenous migration, they followed their hearts up the mighty Murray River back to its source, in the mountains. Returning to Falls Creek to share their dreaming and become full time ski bums.

Falls Creek Ski Patrol '82 > BJ, Geoff Boulton, Leo, Eric Hymans, Eric Napier (bottom), Tim McDonald, John McDonald (no relation), Phil Dodd.

RESORT POLITICS

Continuing in his father's footsteps, Eric did time on ski patrol during the early eighties. Being a proficient skier, they'd always call him when it was a hard place to negotiate an emergency. A couple of really bad accidents freaked him out. One of them, off the edge of the home trail and into steep trees, the guy's leg was twisted around one and a half times. 'It was fucked!' Eric loaded him up with pethidine and got a whiff himself. Then had to radio the doctor on patrol for a special bag of morphine to stop the poor guy screaming. They strapped him into a blood bucket (rescue toboggan), evacuated him to the helipad and flew him out to hospital. Eric was always used for the tough jobs.

He teamed up with Geoff Boulton, an experienced patroller on the rescue toboggan and they'd lift it off the ground to negotiate the bumps. Which were everywhere before the days of mass grooming. Geoff skied that thing so fast that Eric was pushed to his limits. It takes some serious skill to evacuate a patient off a mogul run.

The Ski Patrol base at Falls Creek was in the Village Bowl back then and the boys used to head over to the Falls Creek Motel for lunch. Bruce Johnston would be cooking up barbeque goodness on the balcony and Eric would often have a few beers before heading back out on patrol.

To calm his nerves after those big accidents, Eric also made a bong out of a plastic drink bottle. With a cut down cork to make the stem waterproof, it hid in his ski patrol backpack unnoticed. He'd sneak out of view between the trees on Lakeside to have a couple of cones.

A favourite after dark watering hole for Patrollers was the Sundance Inn. Built in the late seventies it had a bar that rivalled the Frying Pan. It became a popular live music venue where often locals would be swaying around a grand piano till wee hours of the morning.

Late one night during the winter of '81, Eric got into a defensive argument with a guy who was hassling everyone suspected to be using drugs. A biker from Adelaide, who was a regular guest staying in Four Seasons, was brazenly accused of being the supplier. Things got really heated but the crowd sorted things out and security removed the troublemaker out the front. To keep the conflicting parties separated, the manager advised Eric and his friend to leave out the top door, onto Diana Trail, after everything had cooled down. They made it back to Four Seasons at around 3am without further confrontation.

The next morning that troublemaker was found on the driveway below an exit ledge, with devastating head injuries from his fall, he was blue but still breathing. It turned out he was an undercover policeman. Investigations ensued. Eric's reported involvement in the previous nights altercation put him immediately as a main suspect. That policeman sadly died without regaining consciousness.

Then homicide arrived on the scene. Eric was called off ski patrol for questioning. The bouncers were under fire too, from their reputation for bashing people. Crawl prints in the snow on the ledge indicated the guy had fallen off by accident – there was a lack of evidence to charge anyone. Eric's blood boiled from the heat of all the accusations and it wouldn't be the last time police gave him grief. Sometimes it's not cool to be the bad boy around town.

The skier took his frustrations out on the mountain and it was that year Eric won his first official Australian Championship. Skiing took him away from all the crap. He scored another National Moguls Title the following year. Pushing Team Red to podium dominance.

In '83 there was a big change in Falls Creek with the lift company's new owners. They wanted to make everything nice and proper, so they got rid of a few ski patrollers before the start of the season, Eric and another two. Lynne lost her volly patrol position as well. Plus a few mechanics were axed too, who were also displaying the casual boy-next-door look rather than the new professional standard.

Eric thought his sacking was all about poor public appearance. Their uniform was one issue, the jacket was fine but no pants fitted him, as they were all too baggy. He preferred to wear his own ski pants with sponsor logos, Look and Lange, down the leg. It didn't match the new company style. Often he'd walk out smoking a cigarette, unshaved - not a good impression. They wanted clean-cut professionalism, so he wasn't rehired.

BORN TO FLY

Eric styling up on the summit Falls Creek. Damien Pierce photo

The theme of not following the rules or protocol was liberating for Eric, and for freestyle skiing as a whole, but not for his place in a structured society. Eric had his lift ticket taken off him a number of times for reckless skiing. Which he found laughable because he always felt in control, just skiing fast. He believed he knew his line and could react to anything in the blink of an eye.

One time he bumped a senior ski instructor over. A round rosy-cheeked Austrian guy of staunch character called Rudi. Eric was coming down the Summit bumps when Rudi came out of the trees with his private class, straight across the mogul line. Eric came down at sixty kilometres an hour and tried to turn at the last second, but hooked a tip of Rudi's skis. Rudi fell instantly. Eric was pissed off because there was a slash on his ski boot from the steel edge of Rudi's ski. He didn't fall himself but he told Rudi off in front of the class, 'Rudi, come on mate, where's your mountain etiquette?' while Rudi was down on the ground scratching to get up. Eric's ski pass was confiscated again. In hindsight he had to laugh. Rudi has since passed on, may he rest in peace and be reborn with good karma.

Those who know the legendary International Poma at Falls Creek might be privy to how it often got left on idle during the night to prevent the cable freezing. With nobody checking tickets, Eric was one of those guys who would self-load and go sunset skiing or night skiing when the moon came out. Knowing the mountain like the back of his hand, he'd venture out with other keen skiers.

Sometimes they did illegal tree cutting to create new lines to secret stashes that weren't on the map, around The Maze, Valley of the Moon and Wishing Well. Was Eric cheeky, mischievous, or just making himself at home in a place where he'd become part of the furniture? He was certainly following his love of scoring fresh tracks and flowing down the mountain.

Taking some lodge guests skiing after his lift pass was reinstated, Eric took them to one of his favorite spots where the trees insisted on quick turns. Showing off as usual he got too big for his boots, caught an edge and ended up hanging from a snow gum like a koala - that made them laugh. In an attempt to re-inflate his ego, he skied so fast down the bottom of the International run that he failed to pull up in time and slammed smack bang into the lift station at the bottom. He hit the hut so hard that it scared the shit out of a classic Lift Company mechanic called Irish, who was inside working at the time. Tools fell off the racks and everything. The whole lift queue gasped at first, then cheered after Eric got up unharmed. Irish came out and told him to 'Slow the fuck down!'

The International Poma was famous for its unique directional change half way up that whipped skiers around a corner. This was the place where Eric used to do poma-copters to show off. He'd hockey stop to load the stick spring and then release into the air to spin a helicopter while still on the lift. One time the cable derailed (came off the pulley) and the lift immediately stopped.

Eric figured it was broken and went off to ski the Village run and Summit T-bar. After a bunch of laps he stopped at Fryers for a drink and was grabbed by a lift supervisor, who had been chasing him for over an hour but couldn't catch him. A stern lecture was delivered about how pomacopters derail lifts and he better not do it again.

Another penance throughout Eric's life was delivered in his desire for romance. There were love crushes on women that he yearned for, but was always at a loss on how to court them. The ease he had in scoring sex with girls, who glorified his persona, was unfulfilling. The real heart connections with unconquered female friends weighed heavily on his unspoken discontent.

As the eighties rolled forward, things started to get even more frustrating for our local hero, with changes occurring across the skiing landscape. The Peter Stuyvesant Freestyle Tour had finished. A short supply of events that came after that era didn't have the level of sponsorship for professional prizes. Freestyle competition started to be annexed by the Federation of International Skiing and strict guidelines or rules were introduced. Conflict transpired between the innovators and the institutions.

The massive growth of hot-dogging, since Eric got involved in the early seventies, also saw the emerging freestyle sport set its sights on entering the Olympics. Skiers who wanted to compete for gold had to be of amateur status, which created a wide range of confusion for anyone who had previously skied professionally.

Eric Hymans and Bobbi Dunphy. Kerri Darby photo

The great Randy Wieman, who organised the Peter Stuyvesant Tour in Australia and started the official Range Rover Australian Freestyle Ski Championships of '81, inadvertently spawned the 'Brothers of Darkness'. Where skiers vying to make the Olympics would enter cash events under false names wearing masks to earn money. Randy had thrown the idea into passing conversation as a joke and some champion skiers at the time played it out. The state of freestyle's incertitude in the evolution of skiing brought about vicious debate on who was the best and how they could survive in an amateur sporting world.

When Eric skied, he felt like a rebel with a cause. Challenging everything. Growing up he never lived the 'normal life' - with mum and dad or Christmas dinners. His folks celebrated with their kids on different occasions, but their flexible parenting allowed Eric to have an independently righteous upbringing. For Eric it was an epic life. His skiing naturally followed suit and was all about being free, going where nobody else goes, doing what nobody else does, cliffs or whatever. He smashed preconceived ideas about pushing the limits on what was considered possible. Eric Hymans was a game changer who copped heavy criticism for being different and not following the rules.

While children worshipped him, the stiffs didn't like him one bit. Shit stirrers teased his family name by calling him 'Buster', after a seventies band called 'Buster Hymen and the Penetrators' in Melbourne. They were sexually promiscuous times and Eric skied with comical humour.

Eric Hymans (left) jumping snow gums with Rob Bradley. Falls Creek mid '80s

On the tips of a pair of favourite skis he wrote a name tag, like ski school did, that said Erec Sean Hymen, hinting 'erec-tion.' Skiing was of course euphoric like sex.

One spring all the crew headed up to ski the backside snow drifts of Mount Mackay. Camping out at the Tawonga huts for a few days. They lit a big campfire and everyone got on the mushrooms. On the first night Lynne jumped into a sleeping bag with another good mate and Eric's heart crumbled in the moonlight. The rebelliousness of the times meant non-exclusion in relationships but part of him wanted to be with the one. After some wildly influential years together as lovers, Eric and Lynne's dedication to freestyle skiing saw them move in parallel. While emotional details have proven hard to uncover, they both remained close friends and started seeing their skiing lives as having some lasting benefit to a new generation of freestylers.

Lynne learned a bit about marketing from her skateboarding days and set out to create the mogul event they'd been talking about for Falls Creek, to showcase the talents of freestyle skiing. Eric's baby was Team Red, he could see it as a business entity earning more substantial sponsorship that could pay skiers a salary to progress and promote the sport. Both Lynne and Eric would face some serious challenges as the future unfolded.

During that next autumn some acquaintances figured it a good marketing idea to offload a few ounces of pure cocaine into Eric's lap, which they had smuggled back from Bolivia. 'It's good stuff, just fix us up later.'

Well, if shit wasn't already wild enough it was certainly about to go up a level or ten. When recounting Aussie skiing history some have marked this point as being where Eric Hymans' amazing abilities on a pair of skis became unhinged. One of Falls Creek's favourite freestyle ski pioneers would struggle to stand on top of a podium again, but the charisma of the man would sky rocket to unfathomable proportions. By the end of that year Eric owed a lot of money and had to work it off in a Melbourne restaurant. Luckily, he was a gun at hospitality and the hardest worker anyone had ever seen.

Let's not make any hasty assumptions at this stage of the story because Eric was not shy in regards to the use of substances or their abuse. Family trauma or social problems can prompt people to self medicate with drugs, and without proper support or guidance in this realm things often tip over the edge. No doubt Eric had rubbed a white dusty finger between his gums and lips before and used hypodermic needles. He was not shy about living outside of the law. Like so many have said, illicit drugs were mostly recreational for Eric, with his real challenges to be faced in a battle with alcoholism (yes, the legal stuff). Let us review briefly our hero's character – a wild man, no rules, unique and traumatic upbringing, well-to-do genes, a family full of big hearts and war-scarred parents.

To be fully immersed in the times where this story is set – it was a righteous revolution out there! Unprecedented changes were taking place. A new extreme breed was pushing the envelope across a variety of genre.

As well as in every aspect of their lives. We are talking about a period in history when actions, perceptions and technology started accelerating at an increasingly higher rate every single day. There was no lore or limits out on the fringes of society, above the snow line, or anywhere else on the extremities of existence. Drinking and drug use were rampant, and so was alcoholism and addiction.

A guy who worked for Ore Frueauf, one of the founding fathers of Falls Creek (who originally started with Bob at Grand Coeur), recalled having to load the freezer with a fresh bottle of vodka each night so Ore could down a few ice-cold shots before breakfast. The pioneers who created these places were loose, or crazy, or special in their own way.

It's interesting Bob Hymans didn't drink or smoke. Being utterly deprived of everything during the war seemed to set the stage for his boy to live out the opposite psychology of all the things repressed in him. Can anyone even begin to imagine what it was like for Bob, to grow up so privileged and then be stripped to nothing as a Japanese POW? Eric had his reasons to be who he was. Wild men were however just part of the equation.

If anyone can perfectly remember what happened in Australian ski towns during the seventies and eighties then they probably weren't actually involved. It was one huge party back then, seven nights a week, season opening till season close. Then everybody had to go on a big long holiday to detox or rehabilitate.

Eric Hymans on the far left at a Sundance dress up party. Kerri Darby photo

From a few people who still have their health, there are flashbacks of sex in public under pool tables and out front of toilets, swinger parties in hot tubs, beer and food fights of epic proportions, not to mention all-in fist fights when things got totally out of hand. Blood, guts and carnage. There were opium dens where illegal immigrants hid away from racism, acid trips eaten like lollies, and most young people did drugs of some description. Yes, outrageously deranged times that parallel Hunter S. Thompson's gonzo storytelling about *Fear and Loathing in Las Vegas*. This read you are absorbed in right now is a savage journey to the heart of a freestyler's dream.

Toward the mid eighties when Eric worked at the Sundance, he was fired for rolling a joint in his room after the boss pulled a surprise inspection. Smoking pot was an accepted practice as long as staff went outside. Eric wasn't smoking but that didn't matter. The tone in his voice is again laced with bitterness and confusion, because he believed everyone who was anyone at the time didn't mind a little dance with Mary Jane now and again. Plus he had witnessed his boss sniffing cocaine and imbibing many other substances, which had become social norms. To Eric it was a convenient excuse birthed from a hidden agenda.

There was a natural concern about an increase in needle use with the aids epidemic and how frenzied the late night party actually was across the village. Eric's wildness was certainly uncontainable and that itself exposed fear in the minds of those who sought to control the magic.

Team Red in stark contrast voted Eric their official captain coach, which demonstrated his credibility. He made a public apology for any indiscretion and donated two hundred dollars to the race club to appease community disappointment in their hero. Smoking joints may well have been socially acceptable in many circles, avant-garde for the Hymans, but in the eyes of the establishment it was simply illegal. We could debate the benefits of legalisation and education, as in Amsterdam, verses banning substances until the cows come home. The crunch was that Team Red promoted the community and the Sundance Inn was one of their sponsors.

The air was thick with the unfairness or hypocrisy associated with the official disdain of the whole drug culture, while at the same time unconsciously promoting the *Ski All Day - Party All Night* resort. Eric got the feeling he was 'blamed every time a kid at Falls started smoking pot', but marijuana was possibly the least harmful of substances going around during those times.

Drink spiking was commonplace and nobody knew for sure what concoctions made up the pills or powders being ingested. Eric put his views on the effectiveness of making things illegal in a way that only he can, 'It's like a father telling you not to sleep with his daughter, umm... ok... I won't.' [rascally laughter]. With reverse psychology - the easiest way to get a child to do something is to tell them not to do it. In a world where humans can do anything, telling anyone they can't seems down right ludicrous.

Prohibition didn't work for America in the 1930s, it just fueled the Mafia, you've got to wonder why anyone thinks it's going to work for other things. Education is the answer.

We have to remember the mountain scene in those days had no social boundaries, no sheriff and no law. Guys like Eric were simply good at everything going on in his community. Due to some of that behaviour being unhealthy, there was bound to be a point in time when various managers attempted to curb staff conduct, seeing excessive partying at odds with work performance. Which just goes down the road of controlling others and against a freestyler's doctrine. One powerful comment received about Eric's character was: 'The only people who may have had a bad word to say about Eric Hymans, would be managerial types who are in the ski industry for the wrong reasons.'

Eric wasn't about to slow down. One can wonder if all the poking and prodding by the establishment didn't have the same effect as stoking a fire. Heck, why not throw a big can of fuel on it and see if it will explode? Eric Hymans' fire might have been burning since childhood, but as his story is pieced together it seems to have some significant parallels with many other free spirited folk who have been martyred. It would be far more beneficial if the energies of champions like Eric could be harnessed to inspire young and aspiring freeriders to live their dreams. Programs of balance practice and mentoring up and comers significantly benefit these industries while ensuring those ex-champions don't fall into the cracks. It's time to end the suicide.

Eric Hymans with Fozzie, in Ange's backyard (Kent's mum), Melbourne 1987. DP

SKI BROTHERHOOD

For all his laid back team orientated attitude Eric was also a competitor. He wasn't always viewed as the best skier on the hill because he didn't mind falling over trying new things. Experimenting was part of the game. In the friendly competitions between the best skiers on the mountain however, he truly excelled. While others were blowing out, he'd be pulling together his best runs when the competitive spirit was highest. Eric Hymans was a very special type of character among the skiing fraternity during the adolescence of freestyle.

Bruce Johnston first met Eric playing pool with Peter Williams down at the Sundance Inn. Bruce was new on the hill and laid a coin on the table to challenge the next game, before introducing himself. Eric told him to, 'Fuck off,' the pool table was reserved for their crew. Being a punk themed night with everyone dressed up, Bruce approached the boys for a laugh because he felt like a friendly game of stick. Eric threw his beer in Bruce's face and repeated his instructions. Unperturbed, Bruce retreated to the bar and bought a jug. Walked back calmly then poured the whole thing over Eric's head. Everyone thought a fight was about to erupt before Eric cracked a smile. Bruce and Eric have been close mates ever since.

There was always a talent show, open mic, or themed night going on at the Sundance or Fryers back then because people came up from the city to specifically get weird. With everyone on stage for the punk night prize draw, it was indicative of the times when Bruce pissed (urinated) on Pete's leg after he won the best costume award. The next day of course everyone was out on the hill bashing bumps together and pulling stunts to show off.

Geoff Dyke had a laugh about when he formally met Eric. Standing outside the Hub with his shimmering Team Red one-piece suit pulled down and wrapped around his waist. Leaning against the wall smoking a cigarette, t-shirt rolled up with a packet of Stuyvo filters under one sleeve and his Rolling Stones tattoo showing. Eric was just hanging out, seeing who's who at the start of the season. Geoff was thinking, 'This guy is enigmatic in a special sort of way'. Eric and Geoff hung out skiing quite a bit after that because Geoff would chase all the Team Red guys.

A real sense of brotherhood was evident during those days. There's something about being balanced and connected to nature that gives one a feeling that everybody on Earth is family. If someone spoke or acted to the contrary then it's in a freerider's DNA to do something to bring everyone back to the bigger picture of connectedness. Often that was simply posing questions as to why we have separation, greed, or war?

Eric was cool, but underneath he wanted friends and approval – perhaps what he never really got from his father.

He had a lovable laugh and was one of those adorable characters in ski history. Eric was a proper ski bum. Bald tires on borrowed cars on mountain roads, always life threatening and so easy to get sucked into the vortex. Geoff followed the Falls crew to Verbier that year and remembered when Eric picked up his Lange ski sponsorship. Downstairs in guest services, he went over to Dale and declared, 'Oh my god these skis are good, I was turning so fast my brain couldn't keep up.' Eric had that hilarious *je ne sais qu'à* quality about him.

Everyone brings a certain characteristic to life and Eric's was like a Johnny Hallyday sort of suave. French rocker, biker jacket, side burns, sunglasses and smokes, living like a rock star - a lovable rogue. He was a great skier, there were some better, but Eric was a real personality. The legend was bigger than the man. He didn't 'give a fuck' if someone was objectionable about him being Mick Jagger on skis, or couldn't understand what was going on. He carried a special aura. Eric had a generous spirit, always accepting if people came from different backgrounds. He understood hardship and alienation better than most and fought for a better world.

Falls Creek's controversial slogan during the 80s was indeed *Ski All day - Party All Night*. Showing everyone a good time on the mountain was as important as skiing for guys like Eric. When he worked at the Sundance Inn full-time, where big touring bands came to play live music, the fire of his rock'n'roll teenage years reignited. He talked about living with Marcus Lovett like they were famous.

Gynaecologist - Dr Hymans and Sex Therapist - Dr Lovett. Sundance 1984 - KD

Marcus joined Team Red from Bendigo in '83 and won the '84 combined Australian Championship. He became Australia's top aerialist for about a decade. Placed 10th in aerials at Calgary Olympic Games. Got to 4th in World Cup and was a top seed (top 16) Aerialist in the late 80s. Marcus then became ASF coach of the year for getting Kirstie Marshall to her first World Cup win.

The Sundance room Marcus and Eric shared was set up for four people but it was just for them, through Team Red sponsorship. So they pushed the two bunks together for double beds and put a sign on the door that said, *'Sex Therapist - Dr Lovett'* and *'Gynaecologist - Dr Hymans'*. Their place became a legendary bachelor pad with antics built on camaraderie. They'd get up to mischief chasing girls at night and taking them back to their room, lucky the bunks didn't break under that tandem action. During that season Eric taught Marcus about coffee. Marcus always had milk with his and only drank it occasionally. Eric had a little stovetop espresso maker for his morning ritual. Marcus fell in love with coffee culture.

Marcus loved training with Eric, or as he and many called him back then, Wongy, because Eric's style was a bit like Wayne Wong - sit back and jet turn. They'd lap the Summit T-bar on the best mogul run in Australia and ride together. Living freestyle through adrenaline filled days on the mountain with all the crew. Eric's skiing technique was very French but he had a lot of flair and that's what made him so appealing to watch.

Although, sometimes Eric cared more about how the ski suit fitted him and made his arse look, than about improving his skiing. Fashion became an important marketing tool in the snow industry and Eric Hymans was all about attracting people to freestyle.

On a similar level as all individual balance pursuits - skiing strengthens the relationship with body and soul to the world around. It encourages participants to shut down the dominance of their conscious mind, to feel the flow and open their heart to the connection of all things.

This is possibly one reason why Eric has been accused of being 'generous to a fault', which is a trait that may also have rubbed off from his father. With a reluctant grimace visible in the line of his mouth, Eric expressed disappointment about Bob helping his mates more than him. Bob made Eric work hard for everything. He spoke about raising sponsorship to attend the ANZ International Freestyle Championships in New Zealand without Bob's help. When Kent didn't have enough support to go, Bob offered to help by sponsoring Kent's airfare. Eric couldn't help feeling neglected again.

Did Bob deliver tough love to his son in an old fashioned attempt to make him strong and independent? Had he restricted cash flow so as not to be wasted on the party scene? Was Bob really a Jewish miser or scrooge with flashes of uncalculated generosity? Maybe helping Eric's mates might have been a chance for Bob to underpin his son's world without spoiling Eric?

Could it have been an opportunity to support local freestylers in the promotion of Falls Creek as a whole? Eric's guess is as good as anyone's. The only thing certain is a high level of heartache and disorder within Bob and Eric's personal relationship.

    On the road and away from his father, Eric was his own king. There were six skiers representing Australia on that NZ trip and they all stayed at a house in Methven. Eric was the elder out of Marcus, Kent, Martin Rowley and a couple of Thredbo lads. The Australian Ski Federation had sponsored the beds and a rental car. It's always a mission to get on and off the hill in New Zealand because there is no on-mountain accommodation. Getting to the mogul course early meant everyone needed quiet nights before the event. Then drama started unfolding.

    Their accommodation was not far from the local pub. Like a scene from the movie *Once Were Warriors*, a bunch of drunken larrikins suddenly burst into their backyard seeking shelter from an angry Maori on the warpath. These tourists had gotten lippy at the bar with some locals and a death chase eventuated. Eric got out of bed to sort out the shenanigans, just after Kent had let the panic-stricken chickens in the back door. Everyone looked out the window in horror as a giant Aotearoa warrior burst onto their porch for blood. Wielding a stop sign he had literally plucked from a street corner. In an unyielding tongue of anger, this scary native ordered everyone back to bed while he sorted out tribal business.

ANZ International Freestyle Championships. Mt Hutt, NZ '84

Luckily nobody was killed, as the prey had already high tailed it out the front door and were calling the cops from a neighbour's phone (before the days of mobiles). The boys were unnerved by such an invasion of privacy.

    The next day everyone got to Mount Hutt in time and skiing rekindled their confidence. The good thing was that Kent placed second in the event and finally beat Eric, who placed sixth. When a protégé beats one of his gurus everyone has a smile on their face. Eric was a good sport like that. Even though under his skin competitions sucked. They are only good when you're winning and then it gets lonely because there is only one winner. How his heart longed for events that were just like parties, where everyone has a good time.

    Returning home, many kids continued to admire Team Red. Whether they were aware of being role models or not, the Summit was an exhibition zone for freestyle skiing. Everyone hung out front of the Frying Pan and loved the live show whenever conditions were good. It was before the days of winch grooming, when the fall-lines were dictated by the T-bar. The whole area looked like a field of Volkswagen beetles come mid to late season.

    Mitch Smith (co-founder of Air & Style coaching) recalled how Eric was one of those guys he looked up to as a grom. Mitch used to sit on Dog Patch and just be in awe of Team Red skiing the bumps. One day he asked Eric to show him a heli (360 spin with skis crossed like a helicopter) and on his next run Eric demonstrated it perfectly over the race line.

Mitch was so stoked to see that up close! Eric was definitely one of the original inspirations, along with Kent and Mark, very sharp, very intelligent, made people laugh, liked cool music and helped kids get up the t-bar. Mitch loved that underlying kinship of the freestyle brotherhood, like Tribe Gonzo at Mt Buller. Team Red was a massive influence on so many young ones and Eric was at its heart.

The infamous Tower Eight Club would unload at a certain point to get straight into the hot spot of the Summit bumps. The moguls were crafted to perfection by the style and speed of the skiers riding them. An aqueduct near the bottom, which feeds the Rocky Valley dam as part of the Kiewa hydro scheme, was tagged 'the race line'. The best freestylers boosted their new moves off it as a finale for each run. It was all a dance and game of style with two planks strapped to your feet, no one telling you where to turn or what to do. Team Red consisted of only the finest competition skiers and the Tower Eight Club was the unofficial extended family that comprised anyone good enough to style the pro lines. Eric was of course one of the ringleaders, a guy that was pushing everyone to ski harder and faster than they had done before. He was considered a skiing genius by many of his peers and shared his wealth of knowledge to those who were smart enough to listen.

Jonathan 'Gremlin go fast Jonny' Allen celebrated Eric's skiing wisdom. Eric taught Jonny the most about skiing out of anyone and Jonny attributed his major leaps in progression to skiing with that freestyle cat.

Eric knew the mechanics of it all and helped everyone around him improve. Jonny confirmed how Eric was very fastidious about equipment and form, and took everyone with him to another level. Whether skiing on the mountain or getting loose in the bar, whatever Eric did he absolutely loved it with all his being.

Jonny recounted Eric's character with deep insight, because Jonny was suicidal at times after his dad died and Eric was always there for him. Eric and Bob actually saved Jonny once, when he was bashed by the bouncers and thrown out of the Sundance. They took him in to Four Seasons and showed the gremlin some much needed love. While the Hymans were a big hearted bunch, Jonny remembered how Bob always seemed to play mind games and replicate his experiences from the war on Eric. The relationship between father and son massively contributed to Eric's overall character.

Of course Jonny and Eric had some seriously epic times together up at Falls in the old staff roundhouse, where Astra is now, and around Verbier sharing digs. Eric stood out in a crowd, could party with the best of them and always had Jonny's back when someone got lippy at the bar. All the ski-bum rivalry between countries and resorts was so fun for Eric, he could always stand his ground if there was any proving to be done. In Switzerland they used to ski with a gas burner in a back pack and do hot knives with hash in those tele-cabins, laughing their heads off at all the looks they got as the doors opened billowing smoke.

One of the third-generation of Team Red skiers, who asked to remain anonymous, confirmed how Eric was the coolest guy on the hill when he came up through the ranks. Hard core, on the rivet, true to himself and an all-round good guy. Along with Kent, Mark and Marcus they always made time to help ski-kids out with whatever.

The Summit was an institution for freestyle skiing and Falls Creek opened the door to a lot of possibilities to push the boundaries on what could be achieved. The place had a real sense of community with the same people returning each season: Everyone was proud of the Austrian ski school program led by George Pirmoser; There were dedicated ski patrollers such as BJ, Stan and Macca; A solid race club inspired by Steve Lee; With Team Red pushing freestyle. It was a real novelty to ski with Eric wearing his orange Lange bang boots. Many crew were in awe of how he skied bumps. Definitely one of the reasons kids got into freestyle. An incredible motivator and mentor, who made other skiers believe in themselves.

Justina 'Bena' Tomkinson grew up skiing at Falls and met Eric when she was twelve. As a country girl she had never met anyone French, so cool, so different. He introduced her to Velvet Underground and let her follow him around. He told her time and again how brilliant she was (something her father never did). Eric was only ever kind and giving and totally wild and incredibly loyal. Like a brother she loved him. He was a little broken and a little brilliant but the best thing about him was that he was so unique, so purely himself.

Form in action. Tim Patrick photo

Bena recalled how as teenagers she, Mike Clarke, Charlie Brown, Andy Mero and the Costa boys loved watching Team Red ski the bumps. Aspiring to be better than them. The kids always headed to the summit after race training to play freestyle. Eagerly awaiting Team Red to get out on the hill after sleeping in. The racers got up early and the freestylers got out when they felt like it.

A few seasons on and one afternoon everyone was congregating at Fryers as the lifts were closing. Mike Clarke was the last to ski down the summit bumps. After he put together the most amazing run anyone had ever seen, an original Team Red member declared, 'We are about to get schooled.' Those younger skiers from the Falls Creek primary school did indeed overtake the legends to keep things progressing into the future.

Off his skis Eric had a different type of beauty amongst the brotherhood. One summer everyone's preparing to go to Verbier again and getting all excited, so there was a bit of a gathering at Bruce Johnston's place in Melbourne. This shindig turned into a righteous bender, like they all did back then, and Eric disappeared into the night.

Come sunrise and a call came in that woke Geoff, tip to tail in Wedgy's bed, hungover with barely any sleep. Eric needed someone to take his skis to the airport. He had ended up with some girls out on the town and they were taking him in their tiny car to fly out. So the crew threw Eric's ski gear into Wedgy's old valiant and a car load headed toward the airport to see him off.

Next thing BANG! They're involved in an accident and everyone's lucky to be alive. With a sense of urgency for Eric to make his flight, Geoff grabbed the ski gear and took a taxi to find him impatiently waiting at the airport. Without wanting to know what had happened, Eric scooped up his gear, relieved, and headed straight to check-in. No sympathies or money for the cab. The boys had to wear stuff like that because Eric was a classic character, a unique one-of-a-kind type of guy, like a full-time performance artist.

Many crew traveled Northern Europe on the way to and from Verbier to stay with Mireille near Brussels. Always such a novelty to heat up knives in her kitchen to spot hash and not feel the need to hide. She was so open minded and welcoming to any of Eric's friends, like everyone from Falls was part of the family. Except when one of them made the mistake of wearing a punk style jacket with Nazi badges. Due to the family war history, it was the only time anyone was promptly asked to leave.

Bob had a Renault in Holland that Eric borrowed to drive to Switzerland one time with BJ and Debb Bowen. Carrying only French Francs they boosted off a German autobarn to grab some food in France. As they crossed the border Eric pulled out a gram of cocaine and hid it under the centre horn button of the steering wheel (standard practice to import the odd party gift). It was all looking cool until a suspicious customs officer decided to search the car. Shit got real serious when he popped the horn cover. Resulting in strip searches and a nine hour interrogation.

They threatened to cut the car in half, which Bob wouldn't have been happy about, so Eric pulled out all his charm to mellow out the situation. Confessing to the stash and convincing them he was a pro skier. Begging not to destroy the car. The others were harmless tourists with no need to be trafficking larger quantities. Everyone was sweating balls until finally released. As they were getting their passports stamped, Eric had the audacity to ask for his gram of coke back. With a few raised eyebrows everyone pissed themselves laughing.

Back at Falls, the year of the big Lift Company shakedown, shenanigans continued. Eric had gracefully jumped back into kitchen work. Helping Bruce Johnston when he started managing Feathertop Lodge. The community was nervous. Bruce was only twenty three and also one of the wild ones. Anything inconceivable could happen and most probably would.

Bruce and Mick Porter were walking some village dogs as a bit of a favour for Dick Humphreys, a mountain honcho back then. So they decided to play a prank on Ski Patrol. Mambo had just released their poo-shooter design, that depicted a cartoon dog blowing music out its arse. They copied the artwork onto business cards. Every time a dog poo was scooped, it would get placed somewhere annoying to the patrollers with their little anonymous calling card. This went on all season. It wasn't until the Ski Patrol fundraising party in spring that Bruce and Mick finally wore their poo-shooter t-shirts.

There was a mix of anger then laughter from the crowd. The whole of the freestyle scene was about making the serious not so serious, playing with life.

That was also the season of the Bolivian coke flood. Most of the mountain got involved in the crystal clear debauchery that made kings out of peasants. Sadly, Eric and Lynne had their heads stuck in the bag and didn't know how to stash. Such things are best on rare and special occasions ONLY - for ceremony and purpose. Those who did it more than that all paid a price. There is no doubt beautiful people have witnessed some ugly parts of history. Let's hope readers learn from them.

One thing about the freestyle brotherhood was support for individuality. Allowing friends to be themselves without judging. If anyone scored a windfall they'd share it around. If somebody got into strife they would chip in and help. The core of this brotherhood stood like honourable ratbags with soul connection that can never be broken.

It's seriously like living in a movie while writing this story. Eric often pleaded with me to confirm details with any of his good mates like Zelk Huren, as if the stories about these times are too unbelievable to be true. When Zelk came up from Melbourne to Falls Creek, he was told by Italian Joe to look up a bloke called Eric. 'You'll find him at the pub playing on the foosball table having a smoke and a beer,' and that's exactly how Zelk found Eric. Since then a lot of people have thought they were brothers, but they are just great mates - brothers from different mothers.

Eric's best mate Zelk with the biggest smile at Falls Creek. DP

They both loved cooking, carrying on, laughing and fooling around. Zelk ended up best man at Eric's wedding. Later he wiped Eric's arse after a double carpal tunnel operation on both hands. Epic mates. While they never really skied together that much, they did party together – 'big time!'

If you know the Carlsburg Elephant beer you might know that it was the stronger beer back in the eighties, six point five per cent alcohol or something like that. Eric would be finishing up in the kitchen at the Man while Zelk was finishing work at the Sundance. Then they'd meet at the cosy end of a bar and get a Carlsburg Elephant. Take a sip out and drop a shot of vodka in and call them a Carlsburg Mammoth. 'Not an Elephant, a fucking Mammoth!'

In Verbier each season they actually had an Elephant Day where everyone drank Carlsburg Elephants. They'd go to Le Pub Mont Fort for pizza and see how many Elephants they could drink. Normally during bad weather when nobody was skiing. Every time they ordered a Carlsburg they'd get an Elephant stamp. By the end of the day there'd be stamps all over their faces. Sticking their heads over the bar to try and kiss the sexy bar chicks.

It's important to note that it wasn't just Eric who was a loose cannon. The entire mountain culture and ski resort marketing during those times was premised upon excessive behaviour. Akin with his skiing style, Eric was one of the best at doing what others aspired to, in all aspects of life. With a sense of soaking realisation, Eric expressed how wild those times were for him.

The thing about skiing over in Switzerland, compared to Australia, was that suddenly the weather would change and all the snow would come. It would dump so hard that the resort couldn't open the lifts at the top because the slopes were too dangerous. Firstly, skiers can't see in the high alpine where there are no trees. Secondly, there's another layer of snow coming so there might be slides, which could become an avalanche. Everything stays closed so all the skibums and tourists had nothing to do except party. Plus the businesses that wanted people on the mountain, during good and bad weather, encouraged it. This history powers the need for indoor balance gyms for all weather activity.

Eric and the ski brotherhood of that era were part of the X generation. In the evolution of extreme activity it was when riders left the ground and started exploring airtime. Undoubtedly another Team Red performer was Mike Clarke, a next-level Falls Creek phenom in the Y generation, who took technical mastery of airtime into the inverted realm. Nowadays it's the Z generation and everybody is flying more than being on the ground. Surf; skate; snow; bike; whatever it is: if a rider has no air game, they're not in the game. It's the explorers like Eric who delivered the platform of knowledge for these future generations to launch from.

Before, when everybody was still on the surface, the extreme sport pioneers flew beyond what was then considered feasible. The revolutionary innovators had to delete the rules to push the envelope on the realms of possibility, and Eric was perfectly cut out to do that.

Much of the negative stigma attached to guys like Eric in regard to influence, injury, drug and alcohol abuse, or mental health, can be better understood if it is viewed in terms of exploration. The same attributes that enabled these legends to fly down the slopes also put them in danger. What is bad or undesirable relates to levels of unbalance, while all that is good relates to balance. It's no wonder why every freeride activity on Earth attracts those who are searching for greater balance.

The seminal extreme skiers of Eric's generation stumbled across a connection to everything. Making them friendly to anyone who returned the gesture. A funny example was when Eric lived above 'la gendarmerie' (the police station) in Verbier with four beautiful Swedish girls. Considered the charmed skibum, he was always chatting to the policemen like they were family. Even while smoking a joint on the balcony, he'd be exchanging greetings over the handrail as cops came and went below. Cleverly when a breeze was blowing the smell of hash up and away from detection. Discretion is one of the keys to freedom.

The Verbier Connection movie crew from L-R Stefan Andersson, Lynne Grosse, Katie Steven, Colin Morrison, Bruce Johnston, Mark Steven, Eric Hymans, Kent Dowding and Trevor Avedissian. Photo by Tony McLaughlin

VERBIER CONNECTION

In the early eighties, a number of the Falls Creek family had well and truly made themselves at home in Switzerland during the Australian summertime. Verbier was a romantic skiing destination that people fell in love with. The Team Red posse joined in the migration and turned heads straight away. Whether it was because they had mastered the heavy Australian snow, which made the light Swiss powder easy to ski, or the fact that the short runs of Falls Creek made for repetitive and concise training grounds (dancing the same bump lines over and over), is anyone's guess. Either way, those Falls Creek skiers made a name for themselves in the Swiss Alps.

Local connections were made quickly and deeply with the whole lifestyle cycle becoming international mythology. Special relationships were forged to utilise the combined skiing reputation of champions and promotional gems. To film a ski movie, bona fide privileges were granted with both Tele Verbier (the local Swiss lift company) and Falls Creek Ski Lifts. If only they didn't have to scam, steal or deal to survive, then things might have been perfect. It was nonetheless epic. Some might have thought their egos couldn't get any bigger, until they started walking around a ski village with a cinematographer.

People noticed them from across the street. Supporters bought rounds of drinks at each bar. And the performers fought off the fans (or took them to bed) while trying to get some sleep before sunrise filming missions on the mountain.

There's no better way to revisit some of those missions than to play the original feature film. When Eric pulled a DVD copy of *The Verbier Connection* off his shelf, he had a laugh at how the movie was sponsored by Blizzard and Raichle while Eric modelled Lange products. 'That's it, Lange and Look, forget about the rest,' he preached his loyalty because they were the best brands of the time in his eyes. He set the atmosphere for the film by organising refreshments and changing the lighting.

With mouth-watering aromas of a hearty stew tickling my nose, Eric circled his kitchen to see how dinner was coming along. Explaining how cooking has always been a spice in life. Later on, when he became a pensioner, it was even more special than it had been before. Crediting his seeming longevity from eating well. He cracked the top off the bottle of Benjella Shiraz I brought over and poured my glass first. Then savoured a few sips of his own. Patiently, he pushed the play button on his remote control and the movie started.

It was over thirty years since Eric skied for the filmmaker. A feeling of special privilege washed over me, to score first hand commentary on something I hadn't seen myself in probably two decades. The film I remembered was a major inspiration to spend time in the Swiss Alps.

At this point I can see a man who had lost some of his faculties from decades of alcoholism and moments of sheer debauchery. Partying like the holiday never ends. The reality of the consequences of limitlessness seem some how out of reach, when watching powder skiing with a guy who enjoyed a large part of his life dropping epic lines down mountain faces. Yet the actual consequences were ever present in Eric's retirement.

The film has some classic ski cinematography. Which felt historic while at once being timeless. It opened with epic powder skiing and Eric dived into reminiscence. In the Alps after big snow cycles clear up, before the resort opens the top again, the Swiss ski patrollers drop bombs and cut lines. To mitigate avalanche risk for public safety. Our heroes earnt local respect to the point where they were allowed to go up there before the ski patrollers. The boss would say, 'Ok guys, you've got half an hour before we head up to start setting off bombs.' With excited smiles the crew would scoot up to Fontanet, Attelas or Chassoure in a big ass tele-cabin, or rattly old gondolas, then ski fresh lines for Trevor's camera.

They would set off little slides and ski them like mountain waves. One time Eric was skiing down a steep pitch and he hit something under the powder. When they saw it was an orange bomb, things got a bit nervous. He sliced it with one ski and put a big cut in the case. Thinking, 'Ahh fuck this might explode?' they boosted to the lift station below the glacier to advise ski patrol about this unexploded device.

Stairway to heaven, Verbier Switzerland. Tim Patrick photo

Apparently not all of their bombs go off, which is more than a little crazy. Even safety and caution have their dangers.

All the performers had been working on movie footage between 1981 and '84. It was Trevor Avedissian's first independent film, originally shot on Super 8mm after he fell in love with that group of talented skibums. On his return to Australia, he finished editing the teaser using a rudimentary splicer and editor, which was hand wound, before screening their efforts in Perisher and Falls Creek during the winter of '84.

An entrepreneur was impressed enough to offer funding to go back and shoot the feature in 16mm between late '84 and early '86. The production story alone is epic. At the time this gang, with Eric in the thick of it, were at the forefront of 'extreme' skiing. It was a good opportunity for the boys to score some free gear so they went shopping for sponsorship. Steve Lee managed to hook up a Nevica deal for the movie, through Paul Goldstein, and the boys drove to Chamonix to talk turkey with the Nevica marketing gurus. It was the standard ski all day, apres business meeting in a restaurant, then getting blazed at a funky bar.

On New Years Eve 1984/'85 George Orwell's dystopian satire prediction about life under constant surveillance had fallen short. Mainly because these ski rats were deep in the black market and still operating. With a boot load of contraband they had to be back at Le Pub Mont Fort in Verbier before midnight, to kiss the Swedish backpackers who had just rolled into Switzerland.

The safest route was through Italy, where the border control was lax. It was snowing heavily as their two wheel drive space ship ice skated out of the Mont Blanc tunnel, through Courmayeur and down the Aosta valley. At the junction onto Viale de Gran St Bernardo, Bruce turned the wheel but nothing happened. They burst over the roundabout, ricocheted off a snowbank and completed a full three sixty spin before regaining control. A kilometre up the pass, Eric piped up and asked if he was imagining things? Lucky-to-be-alive laughter erupted.

Comedy continued at the border crossing. The Italian side sent them to the Swiss side without passport control. The Swiss side sent them back to the Italian side to get stamps. Multi-language confusion saw them back and forth five times. Until the ridiculousness of it all got too much and they started to panic about getting searched. The guards couldn't contain themselves and burst out laughing at the freaked out skibums. It was all a practical joke. Beers were offered and everyone cheered Happy New Year! Their mission was a success and all the boys got laid that night. They woke up to a day of deep powder skiing. This was skibum heaven.

After all the snow was tracked, a few crew flew to London to pick up the Nevica gear and sign contracts. On the flight over Trev spiked Bruce's toast with some LSD and they were lucky to get out of Gatwick alive. Bruce had the gift of the gab so they hopped, skipped and jumped between ski gear distributers around town selling the movie project.

Somehow they managed to score boxes of Blizzard skis, Look bindings and Raichle ski boots for everyone to model. Free ski gear for skibums felt like Xmas.

To celebrate they tracked down Damien Pierce, who was working at the Chelsea Club, and managed to get past security without memberships. Trev told Damien that Bruce had something for him in the toilets and before anyone knew it the three of them were twisted on acid. Damien couldn't stay at work after that so he scored a few bottles of liquor off his boss and they hit the concrete wilderness. One thing led to another and the craziness to follow went from barricading everyone in a restaurant for a drinking comp, to extreme sneaker skiing in a London snow storm, doing powder eights and stair airs. The night ended by playing chicken with moving Black Top taxis on a busy street. They had to stay alive and somehow found their way back to the hotel. Eric wasn't even there but it demonstrates what was happening throughout much of the skibum scene during those times.

It was when fluorescent colours came in and *The Verbier Connection* film crew were the first to be wearing the blinding Nevica trend. Back in the Alps it gave everyone involved a real team vibe – Colin Morrison, Kent Dowding, Mark Steven, Steven Lee, Eric Hymans, Stefan Andersson, Lynne Grosse, Katie Steven, Lucy McSweeney and Jane Van Den Berg all starred in the ski movie. Produced, filmed and directed by Trevor Avedissian of Hillbrook Motion Pictures. Everyone was pumped to be part of the project.

The crew loved modelling that Nevica fluro. If ever they truly felt like super stars it was during those times. English and Scandinavians were drooling over those ski daemons. Testosterone was through the roof. Across the 4 Valleys in Switzerland, where Verbier is the Northern quarter, their antics became fabled. On the mountain Eric was the hyperactive child-like skier of the bunch. Popping all over the place and jumping off everything. He was most comfortable in the air. Often described as a real motocross style skier with power in the palm of his hand. Eric was fearless and really different stylistically from the other skiers in their group. It was a perfect cross section of personalities to make a well-rounded ski movie.

I asked if Eric was ever in a big avalanche? He explained how the film crew witnessed a really bad one up on Savoleyres. Jane, the Scandinavian ski model, went on a big slab that broke away from the mountain and Eric was going too. Mark was behind a rock and managed to grab the tip of Eric's ski and hold him there until Eric crawled to hide beside him. With thunderous chaos they all watched their friend disappear into the abyss.

Katie, Lynne, Colin and the film crew were luckily above the fracture but there was a 'fucking' huge cliff band onto pine trees below. Expecting nothing less than death and dismemberment, their hearts were in their mouths. Choking reality. When they skied down to the forest to start looking for her, there she was still sitting on top of a big slab that went off the cliff like a magic carpet.

The slab had stayed intact and all she lost was one stock - can you believe it? Jane explained the ordeal like watching the trees accelerate past. She managed to hang on top until the jolting stopped. They had a few scary ones like that skiing off-piste, above and beyond Verbier.

A good reminder to do avalanche training! Having spent a few seasons in the 4 Valleys myself, I got shivers up my spine when I heard that story. The Swiss Alps are gnarly unforgiving mountains.

Another time that things got serious was when they were skiing into Hidden Valley, a twelve-kilometre tour over the backside of Verbier. It's pretty isolated and hairy skiing down there and Lynne launched off a big rock and crashed, breaking her arm. The crew went into a bit of a spin thinking there must have been some bad juju around that day. Hidden Valley is not easy to get out of. They ended up having to walk her out over the mountain to the next valley. Where a lift got them back to the village. It was a gruelling half-day exit.

During those long hours Lynne showed symptoms of hypothermia. Thinking she was getting hot she started undressing and freaking everyone out. Eric kept on fighting with her and holding her and trying to get her to safety and eventually they made it out. Hypothermia is a very serious condition and Lynne was close to death in that situation.

Stopping for refreshments at a lonely restaurant, near the far-away lift, the boys noticed an outside freezer. An inconspicuous closer inspection revealed opportunity.

Inside it were slabs of steak and bags of prawns. Focused more on sustenance than karma, a few items ended up inside ski jackets for feasting back at their chalet. That was just one of the various survival scams that went down.

As *The Verbier Connection* movie continued on his big screen, with its dreamy soundtrack by George Power, Eric's memories flash back and he savoured those times skiing some amazing powder with Kent Dowding and Colin Morrison. 'Colin had the strength, he's built like a brick shit house, and Kent had some magic.'

We gauged how steep it was because of the size of the jump turns they were doing. The steeper they are, the more they'd jump. They started a little slide but that's not an avalanche, it's just sluff they have fun with. Eric points out how Kent is skiing a little on his back seat. Spotting the skis not always being together. In stark contrast Colin's are firmly together. Kent fluked his skiing somehow, don't ask Eric how but he did it, his skis are never quite straight and his hands don't match his knees, they are all over the place. Eric was supercritical even in hindsight because he pushed Kent a lot, like Lynne, Flash, Katie and Marcus. Eric's lounge room was drenched with nostalgia.

Eric explained that in skiing there is brute strength or good technique and there is a big difference between the two. With technique, skiers don't have to be super strong once they utilise the G-force and balance point to flow with gravity. It is a finesse gained with skill and experience. Brute strength, on the other hand, is like a fight not a dance.

Smooth style in Verbier, Switzerland. Tim Patrick photo

It's as his sister always said and Marnie from Kilimanjaro Lodge agreed, 'Watching Eric ski was a beautiful thing because it looked like a dance.' Some people make it look like they are fighting hard and steadfast. Some make it look easy and poetic. Eric liked the dance of skiing: hooting and smiling; clowning around; or singing to himself while being totally dissolved in the moment. Soft like water, not hard like ice, to get in the rhythm. Going with the flow is something Eric was good at in various aspects of his life - sometimes it made him and sometimes it cost him. It always meant he was on another level to those around him.

The powder skiing continued on the big screen and he asked me if I have ever heard of snorkel skiing? 'When it's so deep you get covered over and have to bounce up to take a breath. That's some of the greatest sensations one can get from skiing. Starting little slides and playing with them like a surfer.' He closes his eyes for a moment and I know he is time travelling back there. Part of me wishes I could drop into that place and ride with him.

During down time the crew rode toboggans through the Verbier village for a laugh and the movie shows the sort of fun they had. Eric liked to say they 'stole' those sledges, but it was a bit of a skibum custom to take or leave them for village transport. People conveniently left their sledges outside for easy access. When there was no skiing to be done they just picked them up in front of a chalet and took the steepest track to muck around for a good time.

One season, all their crew lived above the centre village and would always use the same route to the pub. Riding toboggans or sliding on garbage bags down, then hiking home. Gradually a luge track formed and they added features by packing snow and shaping berms. Come springtime it became one of the most extreme speed-racer courses imaginable. Crew were either glorified or hospitalised during intoxicated sessions after dark.

I asked Trevor if it was like a skiers version of Hollywood when they made that movie? He laughed, 'Not even close.' They were simply die-hard skibums just trying to do something. The private funding they received only paid for a chalet and a car. Then everybody just kept scraping along, day-to-day, on borrowed money or vagabond scams, to produce the footage. Eric agreed on no regrets because they were truly epic times. The chalet was always overfull. Trevor remembered coming downstairs for breakfast and often finding Eric asleep under the dining table. As wild as Eric was, he never wanted to get in anyone's way. He did some tidying up, shared kitchen duties with Bruce, and put his point of view across about how the lifestyle might function better.

There is an interesting point about Eric's influence working in multiple ways. It made some people rise to new heights (and become champions) and saw others fall from grace (often with a lot of sadness), but it is that journey which showed onlookers what worked and what did not. This in itself motivated new generations to take note.

Both success and failure help people discover personal pathways toward balance. Some get sucked into the vortex, while others figure out how to truly stand their ground. It is all a process of equal-standing, realisation and manifesting dreams. Which relies on overcoming fear.

    The mogul footage in *The Verbier Connection* of course show some incredibly impressive skiing. Eric assured me that Falls Creek was the local hot spot for bumps. The way the seasons flowed combined with the differences in culture and snow, from Verbier to Falls, dictated what the focus was at each destination. In the mid eighties the freestyle revolution was in full swing the world over and at Falls Creek bumps were 90% of what was happening. At Verbier it was about 30%, until the springtime when they held a freestyle festival.

    Mogul Mania started as a prestigious ski bum rivalry competition. Where teams would come from other resorts and challenge each other. Over time it got sanctioned by FIS (Federation of Skiing) and became more serious. Eric shared some glory there and went on to be involved in not only judging freestyle but also judging the judges. Keeping people connected to the heart of moguls. The Swiss locals and inter-European transplants liked these fun loving Australians. With Eric, their French speaking Belgian accented Aussie wild man, was pure comedic brilliance - a novelty of the freestyle tribe.

    Everyone trained hard for the fitness and strength to punch through the limits of extreme performance.

BORN TO FLY

Balls out at Mogul Mania in Verbier, Switzerland

But by the mid eighties Eric was side stepping away from such necessities. He survived from raw natural ability and worked hardest off the snow as a pro-party machine.

Especially in Verbier, Eric literally became a pro-beer drinker. Teaming up with Bruce 'Bullseye' Johnston, they played darts for beer. Championed beer comps for beer. Challenged the English and Germans, who were proud of their beer drinking traditions, to swilling matches of any description and won. Eric Hymans earned a reputation as THE ultimate good-time factory. He could drink anyone and everyone under the table. If there were substances to be abused, he would do that far better than anyone else too. No wonder many people interviewed are honestly surprised that their old friend is still alive. When he walked into a bar or a gathering, it was guaranteed the whole energy and vibe of the place would go up a notch and reach new levels never before witnessed. Always in an extreme fun-loving sort of way. Well, nearly always.

The Opel station wagon they had in Switzerland was like a pinball in the freeride game that everyone played. Bouncing off snow banks from Verbier to Le Châble. One time Eric and Trevor drove to Dynastar in France, where Eric's Lange skis were made. Eric was hyperactive and impatient as usual. Like he got on powder days when he was amped to score the goods - eager to get it done.

Along the road a truck noticed them trying to pass and indicated right, a common signal to make certain they stayed right and did not overtake. Eric read it differently.

In unnecessary haste he pulled out into oncoming traffic. Then the madman didn't retreat as expected, he booted it. Trevor screamed, 'WHAT THE FUCK ARE YOU DOING?' Hearts stopped, puckas clenched shut, and Trev white knuckled the seat (to brace for impact) so tight that his fingers penetrated the leather. Everything went into slow motion. Horns blared and tyres screeched smoke from the other cars and truck in near disaster. With a flood of relief, 'The little prick squeezed the gap.' Swoosh... back into real time. 'Fuck that was close', Trev recalled. Sometimes it seemed like Eric had a death wish.

People the world over were on a path of destruction at that point in history. Cold wars were ripe. Nuclear oblivion imminent. The charge to commercialism was raging in a battle of global economics. Racism, youth slavery and the suppression of women, all under fire. There were no soft-hand upbringings. Becoming a Jedi to fight against the Empire was a serious option, and that's who freestylers essentially were - freedom fighters.

Of course there are the Verbier chalet girls to take one's mind off such nuisances. An essential cog in the wheel of skibum survival alongside real estate agents. To get cash work snow shovelling, you have to know someone. Plus the chalet girls regularly offloaded unused food, drinks and household supplies from holidaymakers. As well as feeding the black market ski school and mountain guide scam with fresh clients. Bruce used to make three hundred Swiss francs a day showing families a few moves around the hill. Scoring a complimentary lunch and freeriding the afternoon because most punters were too unfit to ski all day.

There is a myriad of stories about how crew managed to ski every storm, like drug addicts feeding their addiction. In many cases it was one and the same.

At the rock star holiday mansion of Diana Ross (famous 60s singer), permission had been granted for an end of season mountain staff party on the last weekend in April 1986. It was set to be the party that ended all parties in the global realm of skibumdom. Everything lavishly provided. Strawberry garnished Dom Pérignon champagne was being devoured by weary skiers. As a murky golden sun retreated over the Mont Blanc massif, a plethora of skibums flooded in.

Hot news circulating at that moment in time was the Chernobyl nuclear disaster. Exacerbating tongues in a rapidly growing crowd were wagging, 'We're all about to die in a radiation fallout!' Anxious eyes stared out at a deathly haze across the Alps and some could almost smell the poison in the air. Naturally, the festivities went off the Richter scale. It may well have been the time Bruce Johnston howled across a gathering, 'It's never too late to have a happy childhood, or a good fuck..!' Think about all the wildest shit that could possibly happen at a skibum party... those things you can imagine probably happened that night. It was the last hurrah of their season and in everyone's mind - for life as they knew it.

L-R Bruce Johnston, Eric Hymans, Kerri Darby, Kerry Lee, Trevor Avedissian, Kent Dowding, Bobbi Dunphy, Sharon Reeves, Steve Lee, Colin Morrison
Chalet Filippa, Verbier. Kerry Hall photo

Between Falls Creek and Verbier, springtime signalled migration time for an endless winter and both places became increasingly popular for escape. Every year more and more people cottoned on to the inside word, until it became a mass biannual movement of sorts. So much so that the Falls Creek marketing department actually changed the *Ski all day, party all night* slogan to *Switzerland with Gum Trees,* to mellow things out and promote international lifestyle and spirit.

An interesting comparison is that Falls Creek is a Southern Hemisphere mountain village nestled in a North-facing bowl high in the Australian Alps, with views onto the Bogong massif and under two hours from Albury city. Roughly the same height above sea level and with a similar feel to Verbier, a Northern Hemisphere mountain village nestled in a South facing bowl high in the Swiss Alps, with views onto the Mont Blanc massif, under two hours from Geneva – everything just on a much bigger scale than back at Falls Creek. The main difference is the Australian Alps are millions of years older and have weathered down to a flat plateau. While the European Alps are far, far younger in geological terms. Both locations are almost on the opposite ends of the Earth from each other.

The various journeys between these two locations were all part of the adventure. Enjoying different stopovers in exotic cities, meeting travellers from all over the globe.

Ruling the Summit at Falls Creek 1985. DP

SUMMIT MASTERS

At Falls Creek in '85, Eric was back working at the Man. This time living upstairs with another Team Red performer and a loose character called Slamming Sam. Being head chef he got a room to himself. It was again the go-to place for after-parties. As a kind of excuse for everyone to knock before they entered, there was a dartboard on the back of the door. Everyone was welcome but nobody could just walk in. Eric would be in the kitchen getting everything ready for opening and the others would finish setting up the salad bar, before one staff member would head upstairs. He'd come back a few minutes later and say, 'It's all go!' and Eric would reply, 'Thanks mate!' then run upstairs for a quick one before service.

There was always a bong and mix set up to stay high when things were quiet. After service, during big band nights on the mountain, they would even do 'snow cones' by sprinkling unconfirmed powders on top of their bong hits. Speed, cocaine or heroin, cut heavily on the black market, came and went along with the tides of holiday makers. Mostly it was smoking tobacco and grass, while drinking booze. With the occasional tab of acid, psychedelic mushrooms, valium or some sort of opium based medication. Uppers and downers – whatever anyone could get their hands on.

That's how things used to roll, a constant escape from reality. City slickers came to the mountains to run away from whatever they were running away from and lose themselves. Rich, famous, official, or criminal - locals were often guilty by association. Plus, in the seventies and eighties, there were no cops based on the mountain. One can only begin to imagine how wild it actually was. Who didn't want to party at Falls? With everything revolving around skiing and social gatherings, on a daily basis, it meant you had to ski full time to balance out the big nights. Those who didn't balance themselves through skiing burned out quick. Those who partied less, progressed a lot further in skiing. Compared with the often highly twisted socialites.

Ol'mate Wenz, a classic Falls character, remembered one thing clearly about arriving on the hill in '85:

Eric was number one in the bumps for sure. He earned it, he deserved it and he was definitely a benchmark for freestyle. He used to come into Fryers sayin', 'Feel how hot me knees are!' 'cause they'd work like pistons all day on the Summit. So we'd give him some ice, to stuff into his ski pants, which always melted into his ski boots - what a funny cat!

Eric would then go off to the Man to make Team Red pizzas. He was always doing something. Revving up any new guys on the hill to share what they had. Enforcing a code that made sure everyone earned their place in the family. There is a lot of respect for the bloke and the skier. Team Red were fair dinkum crackerjacks!

As powerful an impression Team Red was making on the ski fraternity, they were just a bunch of mates going skiing. Haggling for the chance to compete and prove themselves. Skiing was skiing and the party was a party. While in-between all and sundry had to work to make ends meet. It was rare to get paid for photos, promotion or comps. The goal was simply to share this exciting life with anyone who was interested and go skiing as much as possible. If there was a chance of not flying North for an endless winter, it was heart breaking. The magic of the lifestyle was addictive and guys like Eric became the biggest addicts.

By the spring of '85 Lynne had managed to get the Summit Masters off the ground with help from Monika and Crowie at Mountain Magic Fabrics. As a successful freestyle skier in her own right, Lynne Grosse achieved the best results by any Australian female skier on the international circuit during that era. Lynne personally developed the Summit Masters event concept to comprise of a dual mogul knockout competition.

The format was exciting to watch. Down a two hundred and thirty metre section of the Summit run, twelve metres wide, with an average gradient of twenty-six degrees, athletes were awarded points based on jumps, technique and speed. The winner was crowned the Summit Master or Mistress, with a Junior of the Mountain trophy awarded as well. The event had the unified backing of the entire community and the ski company.

Over the next decade, Nevica, Pirelli, Daihatsu, Heineken, Swatch, SL Cooler and Fosters would be just some of the sponsors who supported Lynne's vision.

It was one huge righteous party for freestyle skiing, like Mogul Mania was for Verbier, with music blaring and just about everyone on the hill in attendance. Eric was styling as usual. Making it through to the semi finals, where he crashed into the fence half way down. The film clip of his stack made it into *The Verbier Connection* movie.

Eric dropped into the bumps certain to win. Then from the corner of his eye saw some snow splutter up. He's thinking, 'Fuck, the dude's catching me,' so he put the pedal on and let loose. Which was a mistake. The guy had actually fallen trying to catch him and that was the snow he saw. He was concentrating so much he couldn't hear spectators yelling 'ERIC, SLOW DOWN!' If he had stayed calm he would have made the final against Mark. Instead he caught an edge and blew out. The other guy managed to finish and progress to the final. Eric came third and scored the best wipe-out of the day. Which gave him a free massage each week for the rest of the winter and an SOS jacket from Yogi's Ski Mart.

Katie and Mark Steven took the honours for Team Red. The juniors who entered from the Falls Creek primary school would become the who's who of freestyle skiing in the 90s. When they awarded trophies, Lynne played the song 'We Are Family' by Sister Sledge, as loud as their PA could blast, and the Falls Creek spirit hit an all time high.

Steve Lee and Eric enjoying the Summit Masters. Kerri Darby photo

Ken Bell, a local journalist, confirmed that within three years of its inauguration the Summit Masters attracted all the best athletes from around the globe. It became the most iconic event in that era of freestyle skiing history.

In an unspoken manner, Eric worshipped the wider freestyle family and wasn't worried by not being the Summit Master. Mark Steven was a well-deserved champion and it was great to have locals win the event. As a bit of a shit stir the commentators called Eric the 'Old man of freestyle.' Which he questioned to some extent as he was only twenty-eight and felt in contention to win. The label was more a reflection of how long Eric had actually been freestyling – something only now having mainstream popularity!

Those who admired Eric called him the 'Godfather of Freestyle', because he had been dancing around the mountains with his suave and charm for eighteen seasons, fourteen back-to-back, and seen more than most. He and Lynne had birthed Team Red and were proud as punch of their crew's stoke. Lynne was now an organiser of something completely epic, after officially retiring from competition. Finally Team Red was receiving a full kit of free ski gear. There was a lot to be grateful for. These were the good times, so that night they partied like it was nineteen ninety-nine.

Craig Moegel, eldest son of Yogi, remembered how all the local kids grew up ski racing. Their Austrian coaches were always being so serious with authoritarian accents.

They'd demand 'NO BUMPS NO JUMPS NO HELIS'. While elsewhere, Team Red was mastering bumps, jumps and helis. Of course the kids dreamt of doing freestyle. For the young at heart it was all about fun and not being so serious.

Craig was only ten at the time and entered the juniors of that first Summit Masters. After the event he forgot to return his bib to Lynne. He went up to her room above the front door of the Frying Pan and walked in on a crazy party, with Eric and everyone jammed in there. Sights a ten-year-old kid just doesn't need to see. For a second everyone stopped and looked at this little ski grom in total shock. Craig shyly handed his bib to Lynne, stepped back and closed the door to the sound of hilarious laughter erupting. That was the freestyle scene back then - completely wild.

There was another classic tale about not being so serious. Team Red did a road trip to Guthega for the '85 Australian Freestyle Championships. Marcus, Eric, Kent and Mark borrowed someone's bald-tyre two-door Mazda RX5 with a rotary engine, no exhaust and no chains. They piled in like renegades. Driving up the Kiewa Valley Highway from Victoria, the New South Wales ski resorts heard them coming hundreds of kilometres away.

Along their journey the air gust from a truck, going in the other direction, blew the roof racks off. Skis and torn bags were strewn across the highway. They gathered them up and had to travel the rest of the way with skis jammed in the car. Nobody could see each other or hardly move on that torturous six-hour drive.

With nowhere to stay they got drunk with some girls at the Jindy Hotel and finally ended up in their apartment. The next day was mogul competition and they had to push the car up every hill with those loud pipes. It was classic. Mark won the event and Kent scored second. Stories like this could champion an epic ski movie. Team Red's fun loving persona definitely attracted a larger demographic than racers or athletes. There's something special about being free and approachable, a group of characters that touch people in their heart and make them laugh. The immense business value of the antics of Team Red has never been quantified.

What's interesting about Eric's ski life is that all the time his ego was showing off and being flamboyant to attract attention, he didn't actually believe he could ski that well. Imagine him skiing an epic line and thinking, 'This is shit, I can see all my mistakes.' Meanwhile people keep telling him, 'Oh Eric, you're fucking shit hot!' Most of the time he'd retort, 'The day I can roll a joint while skiing down the bumps I'll be really good.' Part of him felt worthless or unwanted to some degree. He didn't think he was much of a skier, or deserved to be, but there he was living this life. He was beset by the insecurities common in those with absent parents, but skiing was his power.

In '86 Halley's comet had flown past the Earth and a new high-speed detachable chair lift opened at Falls Creek. *The Verbier Connection* feature movie was released and everyone had an excuse to party. Eric lapped up hero worship as a godfather of freestyle.

SUMMIT MASTERS

Getting loose off Eagle Rock. Falls Creek '87 - DP

It may well have been the pinnacle of his skiing popularity. Under the surface another emerging conflict was born from an ambition to get the Summit Masters sanctioned by the Federation of International Skiing and Falls Creek globally recognised for freestyle. A spiritual tug of war amplified.

After a few more seasons chasing the prize, Eric moved toward judging. To put everyone on an equal playing field there had to be rules and there's no need to repeat Eric's standing on that subject. The art of freestyle skiing came from creative action. What started out as an innovative expression of freedom was to become increasingly controlled by established institutions. Eric became the judge's ultimate critic and preached more about personal demonstration and form than comparing oneself to others. Staying true to his love of freestyle, he remained outwardly annoying to the system and anything non-freestyle related. He also remained inwardly tormented. Soon there was a point when the balance between his skiing and partying lives would be tipped.

Partying in Eric's era (and beyond) usually involved imbibing copious quantities of various substances at once. Alcohol is a poison which in small doses breaks down the barriers of fear. In larger doses can numb the meanings of life, make it hard to learn and to love, and cause neurocognitive disorders. Like alcohol, tobacco is initially a stimulant, but prolonged use results in toxic nicotine blocking the action of autonomic nerve and skeletal muscle cells. Along with psychoactive substances, side effects can blind the senses and create illusion.

When traditional medicine such as coca leaves, cannabis, or milk from the poppy, are concentrated and synthesised beyond their natural form they can do damage.

This damage is often exacerbated by a lack of information and education about the negative impact of overuse. If substance use and abuse remains hidden and swept under the carpet, youth can't learn about associated dangers. Drug research over the past thirty years, since Eric's fall from grace, pointed out that policies of prohibition contribute to this lack of information and increase levels of abuse. There was so much that Eric's generation hadn't discovered yet. Maybe it's their journey through experimentation that we can be thankful for? Showing us the long-term effects. Everything has its place but there has to be balance. In many ways using drugs felt like a ceremony to uncover native wisdom. Knowledge that needed to be forgotten by society before rediscovering the truth that there has to be balance.

To rub salt into his already festering spiritual and familiar wounds, Eric suffered a serious motorcycle accident riding home from a party, in the wee hours one spring morning. He injured his back and his pride, among other things. By the time he had seemingly recovered from the bike accident, he was on a plane back to Switzerland eager to continue his Verbier connection.

During the flight, a guy sitting next to him happened to be a schoolteacher who taught French language. Eric naturally started talking to him in French.

Yet the guy couldn't understand a thing or talk back, can you believe that? He was a French teacher who couldn't speak French. Language is a funny thing so they got into a discussion about Eric's accent. Even in Australia people wonder where he's from and they'll guess South Africa or something like that. Overseas some can pick he's from Australia, but at home he's a foreigner to most. His tongue has a strange twist that's not the Queen's English or American English, it's rooted in the Euro-Australian slang from his upbringing. There's only been one time where Eric asked a guy where he was from and the guy replied, 'Same place as you mate, Straya.'

Few recognised Eric as Australian from his speech because he spoke French fluently, along with English, Italian, with sprinklings of Dutch and Thai. Adverse to racism, the mix of many cultures made him proud to be Australian. It was this great southern land where his spirit emerged and where it will return when he passes. After a familiar stopover in Thailand's golden triangle, to break the trip between hemispheres, he was back in the Swiss Alps.

Big snow met Eric's arrival to Verbier. While he was trudging through deep powder, a strong brotherly bear hug from an old friend made Eric's back go click, click, click. Eric was rushed to hospital. The doctors put him in traction for a month and said he would never ski again.

As he was getting back on his feet, Eric managed to pick up a flirtatious nurse and gain some special privileges. Part of which was access to a medicine cabinet.

Eric, Kerri and Brigitte embracing the kamikaze spirit. KD

Always an opportunist, he loaded an empty biscuit tin full of different colour pills before he was discharged. After he got out, Eric again camped under the dining table of their crew chalet. To be around all the ski talk while having space to lay flat. The ski bum chaos was palpable and Eric's dialogue constantly hilarious. A few friends took lucky dips in his biscuit tin and the results ranged from nothing happening, to people turning into mung beans and losing their shit. The pink ones seemed to be some sort of opium based tranquillizers. We could write another book about the drug-fuelled madness that was going on during those times. Or you could read *The Electric Kool-Aid Acid Test* by Tom Wolfe, which was a major inspiration to a lot of drug experimentation in the seventies and eighties.

As one might expect, about three or four weeks out of hospital Eric was skiing again. He couldn't help it because all he thought about was skiing. Things would naturally slow down for him on the mountain and speed up in the bar, not that anyone could go any faster. In his own unique way he loved contributing to the lifestyle and spirit of freestyle skiing through story, jokes and laughter. Eric's influence attempted to decipher the increasing web of regulations and control that ultimately engulfed the realm of freestyle. He was bound by the voice of his heart with its power focused on reminding crew about their roots.

There were still a few more ski seasons to be notched on Eric's belt. At home his entire reality was reliant upon being a gun skier. The righteous times continued.

He lived on adrenaline enhanced with illicit substances and refused to let anything stop him being a freestyler. There was a real sense of bravado woven into the fabric of the times, with skiing front and centre for all those guys. They had a saying, 'If you get away with it then it's not crazy.'

In '87 Eric worked again as head chef at the Man. After a year out of the kitchen running glasses and doing mixed bar shifts at different venues. Damien Pierce, who was studying these elite athletes first-hand for a physical education and sports psychology degree, was cooking pizzas alongside Eric. As well as working with Steve and Mark in the mountain photo shop. Damien, along with many others, thought Eric was 'bat-shit crazy and pushed everything way too hard'. Eric's spirit of wildness however was integral to advance extreme sports to the apex of possibility. Not many people could fathom his behaviour like Damien wanted to figure out.

The biggest drug dealer that season lived in the Sundance. At one point fifty grand went missing from his profit stash and the finger got pointed at Eric. A lot of tension came from that scenario. It made our hero mad because he didn't do it but crew increasingly blamed him. Heavy drug users are often in delusional states of paranoia. An interesting side note is that twenty years later, after the Sundance became the Country Club, a pile of money was found in a wall during renovations. Rats had turned it to confetti but they guessed it was a lot. I wonder how many false accusations were made about Eric?

In the kitchen such things were unsettling for Eric. He was becoming an increasingly frustrated artist and remembered a complaint about an undercooked well-done steak. When the boys stopped him charging out there with a knife, he spat on that piece of meat, stomped it into the floor and incinerated it to a piece of charcoal – 'Eat that you fucking cunt.' This was not who people wanted him to be.

The following season back at Falls, Eric took his food to another level at a restaurant called After Dark. Which used to be above a Pancake Parlour at Gebi's. He received a consumer award for 'Best Restaurant Fare' and looked back at all the changes he had witnessed.

The seven-day social calendar throughout winter continued. During a staff after-party one time the police raided rooms and searched everyone for drugs. Busts went down. Crew got taken away or sacked. The cops knew Eric Hymans. They asked if he had anything but he was clean and just having a drink with some girls. Later he found out a friend had slipped a bag of speed in his pocket as a gift. Sure enough it was there. The gods were on Eric's side but thoughts of slave time were haunting his mind. A relentless fight for real freedom was taking its toll. Wearing him out. The establishment was the enemy.

At the Summit Masters that spring, Eric Hymans came second to his protégé Kent Dowding, with Colin Morrison third and Steve Lee fourth. They were the upper echelon of skiers in Australia at the time. All of them were touring the world for back-to-back winters.

Steve Lee, Colin Morrison, Eric Hymans, (behind) Kent Dowding and Lisa Nicholas. Summit Masters '87. DP

Eric was told off during the Summit Masters because he was skiing with his dog. Chasing him up the old Summit T-bar, then following him down the bumps. Onlookers thought it was cool to see a snow dog run. Some saw it as dangerous. Skiing had signed into the nanny state so they reprimanded him and he had to take his dog off the racecourse. Others complained about dogs in the National Park but Eric had a dog for some time up at Falls Creek because it was his home.

No one really knows if it was the honchos running the event who didn't like the party animal, or whether it was the poisons building up in Eric's body that were polluting his thoughts. Either way many have commented that they could see the burnout coming. Eric was concentrating more on fulfilling his addictions than simply having fun. Ultimately, the real enemy was his own demons.

At some point Bob bought a two-story house in Mount Beauty with the idea of making it a bed and breakfast for Eric to manage. Which could also double as a halfway house to break the drive for long distance guests heading to Four Seasons. The idea for Eric to have space off the hill was a good one and he and Bob did some renovations. Behind closed doors they were both in and out of respect for each other, as usual. Bob was aging and increasingly in need of Eric's assistance.

All the good ol'boys were going their own ways and by the end of the eighties Eric was grappling to hang onto his perceived top dog position in freestyle skiing.

Apparently Eric was happy to pass the baton but others have remarked that it didn't seem that way. In any case Eric Hymans was realising that he had played his part in the birth of Freestyle and a career change was needed.

Eric moved away from Falls in '89. That year Mike Clarke brought home the Junior World Mogul Title and a young Paul Costa stood second on the podium at the Summit Masters. A new generation of ski kids were coming of age and it was impossible to imagine that they were not all inspired in some way or another by Eric's skiing legacy.

Eric had for years dreamed of Team Red and the Race Club joining forces, but a unification between the outlaws and the athletes had proved to be too great an ask. Graeme Cox was a towie during those times and the crew nicknamed him 'Muttley', from the supremely popular *Wacky Races* cartoon. He followed Team Red around like an animated hound dog and panted with his tongue out during the Summit Masters. Graeme loved freestyle as much as anyone and later joined the Race Club as a mogul coach. He laid the foundations for his daughter Britteny to achieve multiple World Championship victories and Olympic success. A few skiers from the early days view Britt Cox (the skier) as a direct descendant of Team Red's original freestyle lineage at Falls Creek.

Mark Steven would be the only member of Team Red to continue competing into the 90s. With the Race Club kids suddenly showing form in freestyle, he decided to carry on the legend that became so powerful for Falls Creek marketing.

He picked up the pieces of Team Red's fragmented dream and aligned with Geoff Lipshut, of Team Buller, to create a joint sponsorship deal between Triple M radio and Bundaburg Rum. Quiksilver, Dynastar, Coca-Cola, Bolle and later Oakley would also support Team Red's new era. This third generation focused on athletic development. It would see increasing support for freestylers to get on World Cup and aim for the Olympics. Mike Clarke, Charlie Brown, Brent Bignell and brothers Paul, Adrian, Simon and Tom Costa would go on to wear red suits. A new breed continued the legacy of podium domination and Falls Creek promotion that Eric Hymans and Lynne Grosse had started a decade earlier.

Eric was proud of Team Red and how Falls Creek produced some magical skiers. For a while he felt remorse and even bitter that he wasn't there personally to direct Team Red into the future. He felt it was his baby and he had seen the vision of what it could become. The Hymans remained great friends with the Steven family and in the end Eric respected Mark's savvy. Eric had never actually finished school and while he achieved limited sponsorship success, his lack of business acumen meant he struggled with sustainability. Mark was a very smooth operator, highly educated and a champion skier to boot. As they say - the rest is Australian skiing history. In your storyteller's opinion, the Godfather of freestyle had succeeded like no other and he should have no sorrows to drown. Unfortunately, that was not Eric's truth.

Charlie Brown and Adrian Costa bombing the summit for Team Red. DP

Eric was over competing with Bob for women. He moved to Melbourne, where he knew people from skiing, to look for a different life. A deeply ingrained misogynistic attitude meant his relationships would suffer. Eric kept hitting Verbier and would never truly fall for monogamy. He was a fun loving, rock'n'rollin' rebel. For periods of time, there was a roster of girls Eric slept with on a regular basis.

He scored himself a great job at the Melbourne Arts Centre on his own merits, being widely respected as a very hard worker, since his short-term construction gigs saving up for airfares as a skibum. He spent the next six years building exhibition sets and props for the Performing Arts Museum and Melbourne Concert Hall. As well as constructing winter ice-skating rinks at the Myer Music Bowl, Melbourne City Square and a floating river festival. He even worked on some television advertising campaigns for chocolate brands, while pub cooking part-time.

Eric also played DJ gigs at the Builders Arms and mingled in Melbourne's vibrant music scene. Constantly in the know about what was going around and helping people find what they needed. For a while he dated a lady called Destiny, who was the sister of singer Paul Kelly's girlfriend. Yes, they hung out. Eric remembered the apartment where Paul wrote his classic song *Leaps and Bounds*: 'I'm high on a hill, Looking over the bridge, To the M.C.G., And way up on high, The clock on the silo, Says eleven degrees... I re-mem-ber...' Eric sung it with heart, a classic guy who put smiles on the faces around him.

Every winter Eric returned to Falls Creek for a ski and a drink. When the snow was deep or the Summit Masters was on. If he was competing he always looked out to see if Bob had come to watch, but only ever heard rumours of his father's brief appearance. Eric judged the moguls during some of the Summit Masters. Haggled with the judges during others. Helped Lynne organise stuff where he could. And went skiing with the new generation.

Some of the boys remember Eric being a start marshal at the Summit Masters one year, smoking joints and preaching. He shared his advice about freestyle form and ski bum life to anyone who would listen. His heart overflowed with love, pushing tears of happiness out behind his sunglasses, every time a Team Red member performed. Those who are admired are followed and mimicked.

Beside cosy fireplaces beneath howling storms, debates raged about the increasing control of sponsorship by those outside freestyle. Where were the rewards for the artists who had created the attraction? Like the sixties counterculture burning flags to reject what came before them, Eric too had rejected orthodox skiing and all the rules to be part of something new. Human history is littered with conflict between innovators and institutions. Unfortunately institutions usually win. For Eric, success in competition was not necessary. Rather, it was being paid to demonstrate the dance of freestyle that would have played music to his ears. Eric always remained true to himself and at liberty to promote freestyle any way he chose.

In 1995 the Summit Masters had just made it to the tenth anniversary before it felt torn from its roots. With Lynne Grosse battling both empty pockets and domestic violence, after so much success, she had to leave Falls Creek. The stoke that lifted Eric and Lynne so high had dissipated and from then on they only dwelled upon epic times. The crew who were interviewed for this book wouldn't change it for the world. Those early freestylers lived their passion and love for what they did through pinnacle moments in time. If they'd been thinking of the future they might have made a living from skiing, but they made more than a story from their lives.

As the nineties marched on, snowboarding changed the landscape of the snow industry. Skiers jumped on the new carving sticks and everything was redesigned into another cultural epoch. Equality swung its mighty sword and now snow lovers revel in a variety of domains. Technology developed machines to smooth out all the moguls and terrain parks became the focus. Jam style events evolved to soften the edges of traditional competition and instant media opened the doors to excitement for all. Still, nothing beats mastering the summit of a mountain.

Lynne Grosse. Bill Bachman photo

Steven Lee flip DP, Mitch Smith heli CB (top), Bena DP, Charlie Brown DP

Kent Dowding mastering the summit '87. DP

Andy Mero JFP, Paul Costa DP (top), Brent Bignell JFP, Eric Hymans DP.

Mike Clarke, Adrian Costa, Brent Bignell. DP

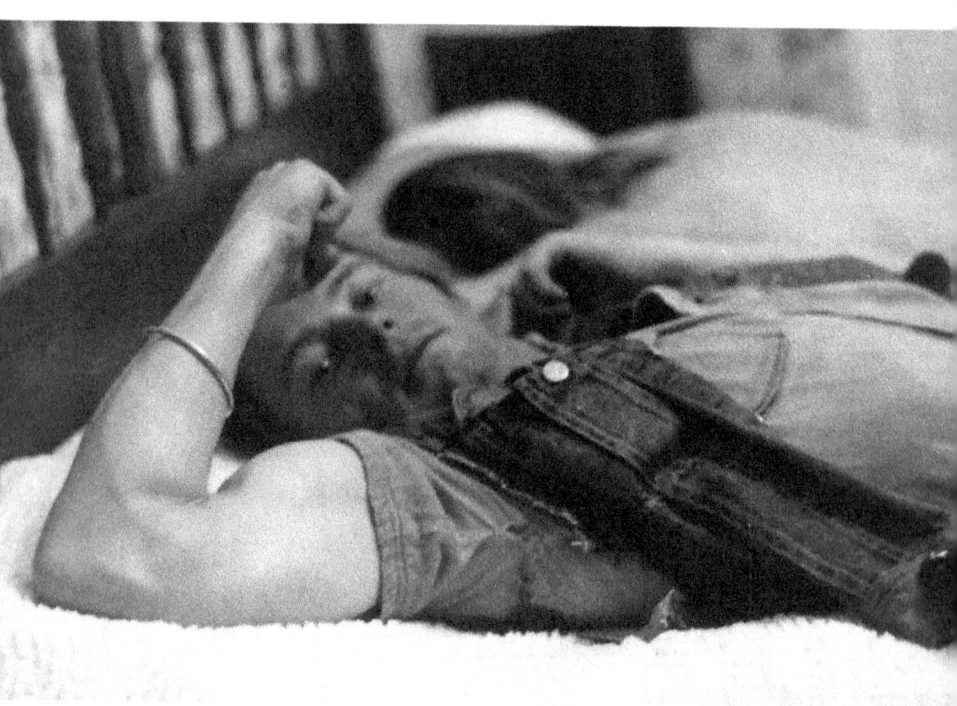

Eric Hymans 1989. KD

APRES SKI

There was one more skiing gig Eric would be involved with. This time for a Jackie Chan movie called *First Strike*, which was partly filmed at Falls Creek. They imported Canadian ski models and stunt men, of which a few got injured during the first week in adverse weather conditions. This threatened the movie production. Since it was such a great opportunity for resort promotion, Bob called Eric to help. He knew the country and how to ski it. The location manager was staying at Four Seasons, so Eric jumped on the project to help build the movie set, handpick local skiers to perform and assist the direction of ski stunts. Being nearly forty he didn't jump any cliffs himself but showed some original form during production. His back and knee were now continuously giving him grief.

The cool thing for Eric was that his old compadres, John Eaves from Canada and local Steve Lee, were some of the legendary skiers recruited on the stunt crew. Eric reminisced about the original Peter Stuyvesant Freestyle Tour back in the day, comparing his skiing life with John and Steve's. It was an internal reality check. Eric was rustier than the others. He assisted a successful search and rescue, after Jackie Chan himself got lost in a white out. They had to follow tracks in full vertigo conditions.

When they finally found Jackie, between a rock and a frozen place, Eric wasn't shy about giving the famous guy a lecture. The director wasn't happy with that but the high country can be a deadly place if you're not smart enough.

Eric felt revitalised by having an important role on the mountain. It was who he was and what skiing meant to him. The movie was a big international project but Eric was always expected by Bob to work for nothing, like a slave. It was another frustrating scenario. Near the end of production Eric again felt disrespected and went back to Melbourne early. He tried to hide feelings of disappointment. An unbalanced lifestyle had caught up with him. Although, there was never a word about Eric regretting his life in any way. His path was his path.

For a period of time Eric swooned women who were his polar opposite. His wild nature was fascinated with conservative people and part of him searched for a balanced match. He explored Buddhism and was adverse to traditions like marriage. Still, he tied the knot in 1996. His wedding night was extra special because it was the first time he ever saw his mum and dad dancing together.

Eric's time on snow got less and less as the years marched on. He spoke with pride about one of the last times he skied in Europe. Eric met up with his old mate Trevor in Verbier when they were in their forties. These two classic skibums scrutinised the peaks of Pierre Avoi to the northwest, after it had been snowing. There were more avalanche barriers than they remembered.

The fear of slides wiping out the village as real as ever. Admiring a favourite aspect, Eric glanced at Trevor and they both said at the same time, 'Let's ski there!' They trekked all the way up and went skiing between the avalanches barriers. Skied the whole face, leaving two lonely tracks, then came back to the village. Deservedly they stopped at a café for tea rum. The drink they used to enjoy as a tradition after a big morning on the mountain. Not tea with milk but tea with lemon and rum, a shot of alcohol in it. Looking up at their tracks, the gurus decided to do the same patch of virgin bliss again.

At the time they could hear people gossiping about who skied there, like no sane person would do that. Some people questioned them, 'Are they your tracks?' and we're not talking about Falls Creek, we are talking about extreme peaks in the Swiss Alps. 'Eric, was that you up there?' they asked him. He replied, 'Na, I dunno, but they're nice tracks.' One can always tell by the tracks if people can ski or not. Eric held a clever modesty that glorified skiing and I got the picture it was that type of cleverness that marketed freestyle so well to his generation.

Eric liked to be the guy who was making others take note, showing skiers around, helping out and insisting crew feel at home in the high country. Constantly sharing stories of his father being one of the guys who started it all. As hard as Bob and Eric's relationship was, there remained a high level of respect within Eric for his father. Bob encouraged the original freestyle revolution and Eric wanted him to be remembered.

Bob Hymans saw Mount Beauty change from the old SEC (State Electricity Commission) town to a tourist town. Assisting the development of Falls Creek skiing. Supply and demand dictated community evolution. Stories about horse and cart trips all the way to Bright to collect supplies, showed the depth of local ski history. Then garages started snow chain hire for cars. Ski shops opened to service snow visitors. Everything unfolded. If the pioneers hadn't developed Falls Creek, with guys like Bob following their dreams, things may be different.

Your storyteller is content that more people will recognise the significance Bob and Eric Hymans had on the Australian ski industry. Bob's name was put on a snow cat, as a sign of respect by the powers that be in Falls Creek nowadays, and Eric laughed because he felt Bob wouldn't have liked it – 'That machine bouncing around with his name on it.' Stories of grumpy men. In line with common ideals it might be great to see: affordable accommodation for the working class; investment into storytelling to share and secure history; as well as career support for champions to eliminate suicidal tendencies.

Thinking of Falls Creek history being forgotten was understandably irritating for Eric. Like a lot of old-timers, he could find things to complain about. Ultimately, to have the freedom that is inherent in freestyle organised and controlled, with its roots of individual expression, regardless of ruler or norms, was Eric's worst torment. There has to come a day when elders are happy in society.

By naming the Four Seasons chalet, Bob Hymans had the original vision of Falls Creek becoming an all-season resort. This started to happen by the time Bob passed away on the 7th of July 2007. Eric reckoned his father picked that day to head off because he was always good with numbers. For fifty years, since Bob's first dreaming, it wasn't viable to open in summer but his vision remained and evolved. It's a sad story of the Hymans clan no longer a part of the Falls Creek community. Will the memory of their legacy slowly fade away?

Eric's dad arrived at Falls in 1948 and made it his home. Bob had block number four and he walked a path to the Grand Coeur guesthouse that he built. Which years later burned to the ground. The original bluestone store of the building still stands as this story nears its end. Bob built a garage for the earliest oversnow transport and had the first phone on the hill. His land was divided for the roads that expanded the village. After that, rebuilding his original hotel was impossible so instead he built the Southern Cross self-contained apartments.

Eric felt whoever was pulling the strings on the mountain kept making it harder and harder for Bob. It is difficult to discover the truth. Eric ruminates about how it all went down. Social sabotage. In 2011 the Hymans family finally sold up for only a fraction of the land value. It wasn't financially viable to renew their lease. Resort taxes climbed too high to service their original clients. The investment to redevelop was out of reach.

It didn't seem right in Eric's mind after Bob passed away. To him there was something wrong with the whole situation. 2010 was the last time Eric skied at Falls Creek. If he didn't feel squeezed out he would have loved to be running his family lodge, cooking for skiers and sharing stories. Instead he withered away down in Mount Beauty struggling with mixed feelings of injustice. He just wasn't into overpricing for profit and couldn't help but share what he had as part of an extended family spirit. As a result, Four Seasons was often in financial deficit.

It's good that school systems are evolving and all types of children are encouraged to embrace education. Eric hated the prison-style slave-training schools of his day and thus rejected traditional learning. It was before kids with short attention spans were understood or respected. Things might have been different if Eric had consciously studied business, instead of circumstantial street smartness, but that's how it was along the epic journey he lived.

Eric's not in denial about how he 'fucked up' on alcohol and drugs, he just couldn't say no in the end. When substances change the chemical structure of your body it can seem impossible to turn off the habits. For Eric, alcoholism is just like sleepwalking back to the bottle shop and drinking without even knowing. The more people judged him and told him not to do it, the more his anti-rule nonconformist auto-responses said, 'Fuck you'. Thinking back on the times he did anything he wanted on skis, a part of him knew that nothing is impossible.

Eric Hymans the freestyler

He lived his life as best he could and had more impact than most. While his dad always wanted skiing to be accessible to everybody, Eric felt resort business developed into an exclusive market only for the rich. 'Everyone should feel the magic of sliding down a mountain!'

In the last meeting Eric had with the Resort Management Board about a potential solution for Four Seasons, he saw there wasn't one. The end of an era had arrived. In classic *French Eric* fashion, he held up his thumb, index and middle fingers to the board of directors and said, 'You get three kinds of people that come to the snow - the budget traveller,' putting his thumb down, 'the working class,' putting his index finger down, 'and the rich,' leaving his middle finger up at them. After an extended pause he concluded, 'And what do you get when you're just left with the rich?' He gave them the righteous bird and walked out of Resort Management offices for the last time.

Eric's bitterness on that subject echoed deep:

The powers that be do not profit from people being free. Freestyle is not free anymore. There used to be a diving board down the river near Rock Pool, in Mount Beauty, and they took that away. Like they didn't want us to fly or they feared for us, or something. I'm not sure why they need to control everything. It would solve so many problems if people controlled their own lives. We used to soar off Eagle Rock at Falls Creek and that was a sweet jump, I remember some great times over that one.

Then they put a fence across to stop beginners falling off the edge of the home trail and in doing so actually killed a great freestyle zone. The trees have grown and swallowed some nice lines. Why don't they trim them back and glade that whole area? It's one of the best pitches to ski at Falls, back to the village. There's a lot of things I have scratched my head at over the years.

Skiing and working in kitchens was all Eric knew for a long time. It was a good life, make no mistake - it was an epic life. He dreamt of future generations taking something from his story and finding true freedom, in the space between the cracks.

Thinking about being known as 'The Godfather of Freestyle', Eric remembered all the faceless little kids that used to go skiing with him, or watched him and talked about how he skied, and said that brought him the most joy in his entire fun-filled life. He couldn't remember who they all are anymore. Showing people the lines and the moves was what he loved, then cooking them delicious food at night. Eric never felt like an old man on skis, or a god, or a father, but he skied for a long time. He still didn't know if he could teach people how to ski properly, because he couldn't remember ever learning it himself, he just always knew how to do it.

Eric often felt like a bad boy both on skis and in life because people have told him off, put him in jail and judged him without knowing his deeper truth. When he worked at the Man, underage kids would order drinks at the bar.

He'd often try to pull them up, 'Hey, you're not allowed to drink because you're too young.' They usually pleaded ignorance but Eric would give them a disappointed look. He didn't know how to explain alcohol is poison that is worse on undeveloped bodies. Even if he had been drinking at that age himself, he's always had the best interest of others at heart. He'd rather see crew eat mull cookies than drink booze, but most parents primarily got drunk in his era.

Skiing was what people loved most about French Eric. When kids came up on school holidays he'd be inspired to ski with them: Katie and Mark Steven at Pretty Valley Lodge; Lisa Tanner from Karelia Lodge; Katie Mackay who became a ski instructor for many years at Falls; Bena (Justina Tomkinson) who ended up marrying Charlie Brown from Julian's Lodge (now called Elk); Mitch Smith; Andy Mero; Mike Clarke and the Costa kids from Mount Beauty; Yogi's children. Eric felt the young ones were his biggest fans because they used to follow him around. They all became great skiers and now their offspring are becoming even greater skiers. Team Red's legacy, to both Falls and freestyle, lives on.

After all the interviews that were conducted, everyone confirmed Eric Hymans had a very big heart. To those who never knew him, his reputation of a reckless irresponsible party animal showed how he became inflicted by the devastating affects of drug and alcohol abuse. This impact led to loss of love as well as ongoing health issues. While his life on the edge furthered the progression of freestyle skiing, it cost him dearly on a personal level.

Life is filled with both beautiful and sad stories.

There are a few people around the world who first learnt how to ski bumps properly at Falls Creek. Eric seemed to hate to admit it but knew he was a role model to a lot of them. His influence wasn't confined to the slopes and consequently wasn't always positive. Eric's insecurities, originating in his family circumstance as a child, meant he never felt confident that he was one of the best. He was hyper-focused on his mistakes. When he remembered pushing Lynne, Katie, Kent, and Marcus, he felt he assisted their progression to become champions.

Eric's battles with his demons meant he only lasted full-time with Bob at Four Seasons for a few years when he first came to Falls. Bob always asserted a lot of control over Eric's attention and finances. He rarely paid Eric for work but would offer him travel and expenses when it suited, and was always having a go at him. This control meant that they would always get pissed off with each other, except when they were skiing. There are not many people who knew the complexity of the connection Eric had with his father. They were sometimes like brothers and other times like enemies, bouncing between the two.

Bob pushed Eric to spread his wings and he did find solace in skiing, like he was *born to fly*. The idea to start a ski team was a chance to soar as a flock with other birds. The thrills, friendships, sponsorships, movies and opportunities in between, were like flight paths that took him along his journey through life.

Witnessing the progression of Team Red and success of the Summit Masters was supremely rewarding for Eric. For over a decade this combination became the most iconic set up in Australian skiing history. There is a great sense of pride about that period in Eric's recollection of his life.

As bitter and twisted as others may have felt during wild binges of drugs and alcohol, no matter how many people got pissed off or offended in delusional states, it was all meant to be. There were no regrets for Eric. As hard as it was to swallow the crash and burn, the fade away, or the friends who passed, it was all part of his journey. While Eric might have been viewed as a broken boy from a broken home, his utter disregard for rules both on and off the slopes were crucial in establishing freestyle skiing.

Eric chilling out with a beer in Seaspray. KD

A beautiful autumn vista of the big fella – Mt Bogong, Victoria Australia

SUNSET

Eric was impressed by the way I drafted his stories, and I was impressed by the way he told them. Together we hope you have enjoyed this read, as well as found a little inspiration along the way. Your storyteller enjoyed a few hearty meals with French Eric and shared his love of simple, honest food. A master chef can be recognised by the way they use their knives and Eric's were sharp. He stressed the importance of eating well and said the thing that kept him alive, amid the abuse, was his cooking.

In the midst of a relaxed dining ambiance, his voice opened magical realms. Like his father, Eric always loved to share stories. Some evoked hysterical laughter, while others permeated deep sorrow, both brought up tears. Of course not everything about his life has been revealed and no doubt there will be conflicting views about some of the details within. Eric maintained, 'Imagination is a beautiful thing,' - Bob taught him that.

We looked out over his second story balcony toward the Mount Beauty golf course, in the direction of Falls Creek. It was a spectacular day. Nature's colour vibrant with late afternoon sunshine. Birds were singing on the power lines. 'The world has changed' Eric confided with nothing more to say. 'And it will keep on changing,'

I replied. Knowing his body may pass but this spirit, which yearns for freedom, will live forever.

After a long time savouring the moment, I suggested the ugly power lines are only temporary, soon to be obsolete, and the worlds we witness in life will flower into more and more beautiful places. Eric hated power lines and remembered laying cable for Telstra, where he witnessed fluorescent tubes lighting up without being plugged in. He's been zapped a few times during the course of his life but his heart was still ticking when we finished this book.

A lot of his mates had gone, some very sadly through overdose or suicide, and after sixty laps around the sun he felt like one of the last men standing from his breed. Those who are still alive were getting sick and couldn't remember much, or 'they were sleeping with a good woman' and had better things to do than talk to him. In any case he was doing pretty damn good considering the shit he did deep in the party scene for thirty years. He somehow never got buried in an avalanche either and deserved a final say:

> There's no snow out there Pete, otherwise I'd go skiing with you today (the knowledge of a skier remained warm in his heart). I've still got the boots and all the gear but we are going to need a car long enough for my two metre planks to fit in (cheeky laughter). I tried a pair of new style shorter skis once but they just wobble, it's not stable for me. Na... I need two hundreds under my feet to enjoy a slide. It's another style of skiing again, a new generation.

They say you have to hold your legs apart with the new skis. Not like the old triangle where you get your knees together and pull everything in tight. So kids are doing things differently and that's great. In the end it's all about the game around your balance point. No bout a doubt it (classic laughter)!

2006 was the last year Eric was going out everyday onto the mountain. He remembered coming down to Mount Beauty that spring and running into Zelk, who commented, 'A few of the boys have been watching you ski and they say you can still turn'em.' That made Eric feel worthy, you know, hearing that from his old mate.

Then he was looking after Four Seasons while his father was passing away and everything got lost. On Bob's deathbed, just before his last breath, he told Brigitte to 'Tell Eric I'm sorry'. Why couldn't he look Eric in the eye and say it? Since then Eric's only skied a few times, mostly hiding away behind boxes of beer or cheap bottles of wine.

I tried to lighten the mood, 'Come on Eric, life's too short to drink cheap wine!' Like a Grand Master he rested his hand on my shoulder and spoke softly out the corner of his mouth, 'It hasn't always been cheap, but it's always been necessary.' There is no hysterical laughter to follow these words. The sheer heaviness of this reality wells tears in my eyes again. For a while I was lost for words.

Feeling a need to change the subject we start talking about the winter Olympics. Like most old ski bums Eric always turned it on to watch his favourite disciplines.

Amazed at the progression that has occurred since he might have been a contender for gold. Blown away by the new aerial manoeuvres. 'Those kids are really learning to fly,' the stoke evident in his tone. Although, he's unimpressed by modern mogul courses because they are all machine made and perfect, built for robots.

He loved the variety of natural bump lines that were created by the way skiers carved the mountain. They were largely unpredictable and therefore required a special skill to master. Eric was an architect of fun bumps, a dancer of the line and loved to catch air everywhere. There is something very special about hearing these tales from a ski elder. Chatting to a man with experience. Sharing stories of times had, lessons learned and questions raised - the passing of knowledge.

Rituals like this inspire dreams of epic centres that hold place for wisdom in the search for balance. I asked if he had considered making his house a bed and breakfast for skiers to come and stay. Four Seasons at Falls Creek was a place like that and everyone used to come to hear Bob's stories, talking about years spent skiing the mountain. People loved it so much they bought Bob presents and Eric really enjoyed cooking them food.

After his father passed away, Eric preferred his own space and time alone. He did after all become a recluse like his father. I wonder if both ideals of private space and community sharing could coexist in a freestyle centre. Eric liked that dream and showed me his little gym and ski-tuning bench collecting dust. The last golden rays of sunlight splintering through the room. Outside a crimson sky spoke of sunset as Eric showed me his boat and car that don't get used anymore, which he offered if ever I have a need. It is true that Eric had a very big heart.

Some kids used to call him Yoda on skis, the wise old Jedi freestyler, so I asked Eric to sum up his story:

To tell ya the truth about the way I was brought up, when I found ice-skating and skiing it set me loose. There was nobody trying to tell me what to do so I did whatever I wanted. That's why I was freestyle, because there was nothing stopping me from being completely free. I really enjoyed myself and that's what it's all about - enjoyment. Just enjoying life.

Yeah I was doing things that other people weren't doing, but it wasn't on purpose or part of some hidden agenda. The agenda was having fun, living in the moment, searching for new thrills. No rules or regulations or any of that shit. The door is open and everything is happening. *'Imagine all the people living for today* [John Lennon], then the guy gets shot. Isn't it a weird world? Australia was once a lucky country and then it felt like a fucking dictatorship. You can't do this, you can't do that - the thing is to respect others and share a smile.

This is my simple religion: There's no need for temples or complicated philosophy, our own brain and heart is our temple and the philosophy is kindness! I got that from the honourable Dalai Lama.

He also said 'Learn the rules so you know how to break them properly.' I've made some good friends with people who didn't have their heads up their arse. Freestyle was fucking great, it was a revolution, burning ya bras or whatever. Sticking ya finger up at the man, just for a laugh. Ya know it was Woodstock in Falls Creek back in the seventies. Get a life guys, there is a great big world out there. Go bust down the doors and spread your wings and all that.

My story is about freestyle, following your heart, going for the thrill and living in the moment. In many ways life was a struggle, lived on a shoestring, but it was all so epic. The years of skiing, partying, sex, drugs, rock'n'roll - some might think it was an escape because Bob treated me like a prisoner of war, or his bastard son, but it was just an exercise in freedom. To be a real freerider it's got to do with having an open mind and being able to think outside the square. You can teach someone how to ski or snowboard but you can't teach freeriding, because it comes from inside. They told me not to do something and I just said fuck'em and did it twice as hard. What a crack up!

Essentially anything is possible so there's no point telling people how to live. It's like going to jail for carrying hash, everybody's doing it so why am I getting locked up? Where I came from it's free-range so I never thought I would get into trouble for it. A funny fact is that per capita there are more dope smokers in Australia than there are in Holland.

I was totally blown away when I found that out. Now is probably a good time to recognise that marijuana is not that bad for us, alcohol is a lot worse - alcohol fucking kills people, it's poison. Tell me about it! I'm an alcoholic and I admit it - I drink too much. You know, that's the way it is. I swapped from that to that like a lot of my friends and the thing is a lot of my friends have passed now but I'm still here. People say to me.. 'Fuck Eric, you still alive?' And I smile and reply, 'Yeah I am.' Even the doctors keep telling me that my body is past the expiry date, as far as they're concerned. Fuck'em, I don't give a rat's arse.

À votre santé!

In memory of
Lynne Grosse
Mike Clarke
Andy Kelly
Team Red

Eric Hymans 2006

EPILOGUE

So, how much of this book is true? Before meeting Eric, I knew of him only as a sad case, a drunk who would help you out if he could. After getting to know him, I was blown away by his stories and strangely aware that he could die at any moment. To learn about the skier that was and the guy who partied so hard that in the end the people in his world dissociated from him, has been eye opening. I learned a lot and hope you did too.

Eric's latter life situation when measured up against societal norms, accompanying the loss of many of those close to his heart, touched him deeply. Eric's response though, as quoted previously, would likely have been, 'I don't give a rat's arse'. Bravado can be a very affective coat of armour. While he's never openly sought approval from others, his life as a champion skier did seek recognition and I got the feeling he wouldn't mind a little bit of empathy now and then.

While putting this book together Eric was living on the fringes of society and always so graciously accepting of his lot in life. Surprisingly enough, he passed away the night we launched *Born to fly* for the *Summit Masters* revival. His legacy complete. This story is Eric's swan song to salute a unique, influential and passionate life. His body did him proud but was no longer in a recoverable state. I can imagine him smiling as he flew through the pearly gates.

EPILOGUE

Eric's story emphasizes the need for flexible education, freeride psychology and proper support for performers - concepts that didn't exist in Eric's world. There was heartache from not being privy to or rewarded for his part in filling pockets, like his soul had been stolen to sell products. May the world finally recognise how important balanced exchanges of energy are to solve problems in society. There are common threads in the suicidal tendencies of great freeriders falling from grace.

Glorifying Eric's life and pretending the success and enjoyment of his youth didn't come at a cost, is not my aim. However, I certainly don't want to pretend it never happened at all. If people continue to ignore the past, I fear the next generation is doomed to make the same mistakes. Pass on the knowledge. Where there is pleasure there is pain and both can be rewarding. We learn from our failures. In the Yin there is a little bit of Yang and vise versa.

Everything on Earth has its place and as such Eric was agreeable to substance use but loathe to the abuse. Black markets pushed the drug sphere into angry and ugly places. Speed and smoking may well have rotted his teeth, but ice was robbing the soul from his community.

Many people told me Eric's life was 'unpublishable', illegal shit and the sadness of drug and alcohol abuse. The repercussions of war are quite astonishing. Be that as it may, to ensure homage is paid to a freeride elder and the need for balance in life highlighted to a new generation, Eric's story needed to be written and *Born to fly* has to be shared.

Ode to the Misfits by C. Ara Campbell via Rebelle Society:

"Here's to the wild, the weird and the wonderful. To those who ride the waves on their own seas and lose sight of the shore. Who discard the rules, the labels and the chains that once bound them, in search of the truth of their heart. To the ones who are fueled by the authentic and the uncensored, no matter how gritty the taste at times.

Here's to the mismatched puzzle pieces that don't get invited to join in all the reindeer games; that get left behind in the dust to learn their own way to fly. Who in their sacred solitude grace the skies with wings of freedom and a destiny born of soul fire. To the rare, unearthly beings who walk the road less traveled, taking the adventure that rises on this path with purpose and passion. Who are brought alive by the fire in their blood and the longing threaded through their being.

Here's to the rebels, the heartsick originals, and the bittersweet loneliness that fuels their spirit. To the ones who won't conform, back down or step aside. To the ones who were not born to fit in but to gloriously stand out. To those who are here to be midwives of the genuine. To the tribe of troublemakers that think so far outside the box, they dream on the edges of the infinite. To those who dance even though they have no idea how; who stumble and make it part of the steps, sing completely off-key and totally out of tune. To the ones who raise their voices to the heavens even though they don't always know the words.

Here's to the awakened ones whose purpose is to feed their soul and not starve it. Whose mantra is the drumbeat of their own heart and the brilliant possibility that looms on the horizon. To the ones who dare to be open, to feel, to love and to live.

Here's to the magical, the mystical and the misunderstood. To the wise ones who move between the shadows and the light. To those who howl at the Full Moon and run naked in the flowing streams. To those who read the compass written on the walls of their hearts and follow the North Star etched upon their spirit.

Here's to the fallen, the broken and the shattered. To the warriors who know that to be cracked is to let the light in deeper. Who know that the best fruit is on the very tip of the branch and the brightest jewels are hidden within the roughest of surfaces. To the ones intoxicated by the burning of the winds of change in their lungs and who live in the lands that others fear to tread.

Here's to the brightly colored patchwork of divine visionaries that won't stand down, play small or sit out. To the stargazers, the storm-chasers and the Old Souls that walk this Earth.

Here's to the wild ones.

Here's to you."

MEMORIAL

Eric Marc Hymans
21.12.57 - 9.9.18

His freestyle lives on in the hearts of dear friends.
His spirit flies high in our mountains forever.

rest in peace

ACKNOWLEDGMENTS

Special appreciation to all those who donated to produce *Born to Fly*: Especially Brigitte Hymans; Arnaud Dalbis; Chantal Hymans; Ben Hudson; Sheridan Alves; Mark Steven; Pedro Ramis; Steven Huren; David Sisson; Rob Sarroff; Kerri Darby; Robin Bayly-Jones; Geoff Dyke; Bruce Johnston; Greg Lee; Flea Stewart; Debra Bowen; Chris Hocking; Jack Langedyk; Shane Johnson; David van Putten; Damien Hamer; Neil Brandt; Sean Oakley; Jim Darby; Justina Tomkinson; Dave Graham; Lange / Future Sport; Traverse Alpine Group / New Frying Pan Inn; as well as our anonymous donors. You made the exhaustive work in this story possible.

Hats off to Eric Hymans for sharing his life, with grand kudos to all of Eric's friends and ski fraternity who did talk openly on un-publishable subjects and hilariously funny happenings. Sharing memories in a way that put me inside the mythology of French Eric. In no particular order my gratitude goes to: Lynne Grosse, Steven Lee, Katie Steven, Brigitte Hymans, Mark Steven, Peter Williams, Marcus Lovett, Jonathan Allen, Trevor Avedissian, Damien Pierce, Bruce Johnston, Kerri Darby, Randy Wieman, Brent Bignell, Geoff Dyke, Mitch Smith, Bob Irwin, Andy Mero, Craig Moegel, Monika Plohberger, Justina Tomkinson, Jim Darby, Robin Bayly-Jones, Anthony Wenzel, Paul Mason, Shirley and Albert Costa, Mike Haid, Tom Costa, Charlie Newton-Brown, Zelk Huren, Andy Shuttleworth, Ken Bell, Campbell Ford, Debb Bowen and Jarrah Kurth, for all your stories. It has been an emotional roller coaster but overall an utterly enjoyable project.

I am so grateful to Lynne Grosse for sharing memories about Eric's and her life, she was a big part of this story and Australian skiing history. Lynne passed away during editing, at fifty six. A beautiful soul her wings took flight. May she score epic surf, perfect sk8 bowls and deep powder in her next life! Lynne was so stoked that we were working on this book. Ol'mates dance again.

Hugs to Kate Campbell for structural-editing and publishing advice; Ian da Silva for line-editing and psychological scrutiny; Maureen Gearon for copy-editing and encouragement; Monika Plohberger for final proof reading. As well as those who viewed the manuscript during various stages and gave feedback. Cheers to Damien Pierce, Kerri Darby, Katie Steven and Graeme Cox for digging up photos. Plus photographers: Bill Bachman; Jeep Novak; Robin Bayly-Jones; Mike Haid; Tim Patrick; Tony McLaughlin, Charlie Brown @ Mountainside; Justin Field, Trevor Avedissian. Copyright is important, please reach out if credits are needed for any unmarked images used from Eric's photo albums.

Love, light and epic balance

Lynne Grosse

ABOUT THE AUTHOR

Peter Corney is a visionary, storyteller, freerider. He has published ten Journals and Poetry for the People, a storybook that put skiers, boardriders, bikers and flyers in the same genre. As a pioneer snowboarder he was criticised for putting a skier on the cover of his first edition. He stands up for the greater freeride family. Peter first visited Falls Creek in 1988 and moved there in the autumn of '91. Since then he has lived twenty-six winters at home and thirteen overseas. Chasing snow and working seasons in the USA, Japan, Canada, France, Switzerland and New Zealand. Preacher of the Summit Heartcore International Freeride Tribe (SHIFT), he is a campaigner for everyone to find their own EpicBalance. Creating photo storylines to inspire one-love and equilibrium is a passion, hence his business being called Epicscope and his moniker - *Pea Ce.*

epicbalance.com

PREVIOUSLY BY EPICSCOPE

Anticipation

winter heat

www.ingramcontent.com/pod-product-compliance
Lightning Source LLC
Chambersburg PA
CBHW070602020526
44112CB00050B/2282